A guide to Historic Texas Inns and Hotels

For Norene and Ernie —
Thank you, dear old friends,
for sharing my new
Career — with all love —
Ann Ruff
5-16-84

A guide to Historic Texas Inns and Hotels

Ann Ruff

Lone Star Books
A Division of
Gulf Publishing Company
Houston, Texas

For making it possible:

Earl Ruff, Delores Keller, Frank Chesky,
Philip Rothenberg, Adam Wolski, Luis Campos,
and, with special appreciation, Peter Morris.

Drawings by Irin Lewis
Cartography and Book Design by David T. Price

A Guide to Historic Texas Inns and Hotels

Contents

Foreword

Ann Ruff and I have traveled many of the same roads. We have stopped at some of the same places. We have been drawn to many of the same attractions. We admire many of the same individuals and institutions. We seem to have complementary purposes.

I have sought to call attention with the *Eyes of Texas* television series to those parts of Texas that freeway travelers, in their haste, seldom see. Likewise, in this book, Ann gives travelers valuable information about places where they may eat and hotels where they may stay while seeing the *real* Texas.

Ray Miller
January 1982

Introduction

My original intention when writing this book was to include only historic and quaint Texas hotels and inns you could actually stay in, but the more I traveled through Texas and the more hotels I saw, I realized that many wonderful buildings and their stories would be left out. How could I write about Texas hotels and not include all the famous old hotels that are now restaurants and museums? And what about the others that were once so great but have now faded into obscurity and are vacant or exist only as retirement homes?

In nearly every town I went to in Texas (and in more than 10,000 miles, I covered many, many towns) I usually found a hotel of some description. Almost always it was deserted—a silent comment on a society that no longer wanted it. I thought of all the thousands of other towns in the United States that no longer cared about their hotels either, and of all the empty buildings throughout the country. It made me very sad thinking of those places that had meant so much to their communities at one time but which have no place in today's way of life.

A hotel is so much more than just a place to unpack a suitcase. A hotel is where many of life's important events take place: the senior prom, weddings, honeymoons, anniversaries, memorable vacations. A hotel is where special parties and banquets are held, and where friends and important people stay. Stars perform in its ballroom, and its bars and lobbies become special places to meet. A hotel is made of memories, and it is those memories that make a hotel great. I guess what made me so sad when I found all the deserted and run-down hotels is that no one cared about those memories anymore.

I have included a section on "Ghosts," which tells the fate of some of these abandoned hotels. The list is by no means complete; an entire book could be written on each of them, for they all were great in their day. The section on the Greenbriar Inn covers those once-famous hotels which are still in operation but which have fallen on hard times and are now mostly retirement homes. The Greenbriar Inn's story sums up the fate of so many.

The section on "Survivors" covers some of the great hotels now used for other purposes, but which have still maintained their dignity. And no book on Texas hotels would be complete without including the Conrad Hilton success story. Few people realize that one of the world's greatest fortunes began with the Mobley Hotel in little Cisco, Texas, nor do they know that the first hotels bearing the Hilton name were in Texas.

For the most part, however, I have written about hotels and inns that are special in their own way. They range in size from the three-bedroom Lickskillet Inn in Fayetteville to the $45-million restored Adolphus in Dallas. Texas is rediscovering her inns and hotels of the past. People are being drawn back to old furniture, claw-foot bathtubs, and rooms with singular character. There is a definite trend away from driving miles and miles to stay in the same room every night. Travelers want to escape from neon signs, piped music, formula decor, hucksters selling turquoise jewelry, and mass-produced food. It is still possible to sleep amid antiques and be made to feel like a special person, and Texas has a varied collection of such accommodations. There may be no porters, no room service, perhaps no phones or TV; the plumbing may be rebellious—or the hotels may be the epitomy of luxury—but each has its own particular charm. Each and every hotel in this book has something special going for it—antiquity, location, nostalgia, seclusion, cuisine, or just plain old tradition. But all share one very important characteristic: their owners love them. Perhaps that is what really makes them all so special.

A few things to keep in mind . . .

This is a book about historic hotels of all types. Most described here are open for guests. A few are just restaurants and several are museums, but all are well worth a visit. Many of them you will want to return to over and over again. However, the importance of advance reservations cannot be stressed enough. Not only do some of these hotels have a very limited number of rooms but they are also in fairly isolated areas, and often no other accommodations are available.

You should also be aware that the rates quoted here are subject to change. This is particularly true of meal prices. Be sure to ask what the current rates are and what they include. For instance, a room with a private bath will be higher than one with a shared bath. Some inns have a continental breakfast included in the price of the room, and in others breakfast is an additional charge. At the larger hotels in the cities, you may wish to check on the availability of special weekend rates.

Many of the inns and hotels have rules regarding children and pets to protect the special charm or qualities of the establishment. A dog may not be noticed in a standard motel setting, but even a small pooch can dominate a country inn. And although one's own children are perfect, somehow that feeling is not always shared by others who want an intimate setting or total relaxation. It is wise to inquire specifically when you make your reservations; most inns allow neither pets nor children.

At this printing, several of the hotels were still being remodeled, refurbished or restored and were unable to give a firm opening date. So, again get the latest information before making travel plans. You can rest assured that when the hotels do open, all will have been worth waiting for.

For this book to continue to grow and be kept current, it is very important to hear from its readers. I would very much like to know about your experiences, both good and bad, at the inns and hotels in this book. As you will note, there is no rating system. Things I love about these hotels may not appeal to everyone, and I may have somehow missed what you consider the best part of all. Also, please tell me of any hotels you think should be included that were omitted, as I may have inadvertently left out one of your favorites. If you find another old hotel, or one being restored, please let me know so that it, too, may be included in future editions. I will make every effort to answer each letter personally.

Researching and writing this book was one of the most rewarding events in my life. True, it was sad to find so many deserted and run-down hotels, but it was wonderful to find so many still in operation and others under restoration. But best of all were the grand people I met who were willing to endure all the headaches and heartaches that go with refurbishing and living in old buildings. They were all so proud, pleased, and enthusiastic about their work. It was a sheer delight to share it with them. I hope you too will share their feelings and visit them all.

Ann Ruff

North
Central
Texas

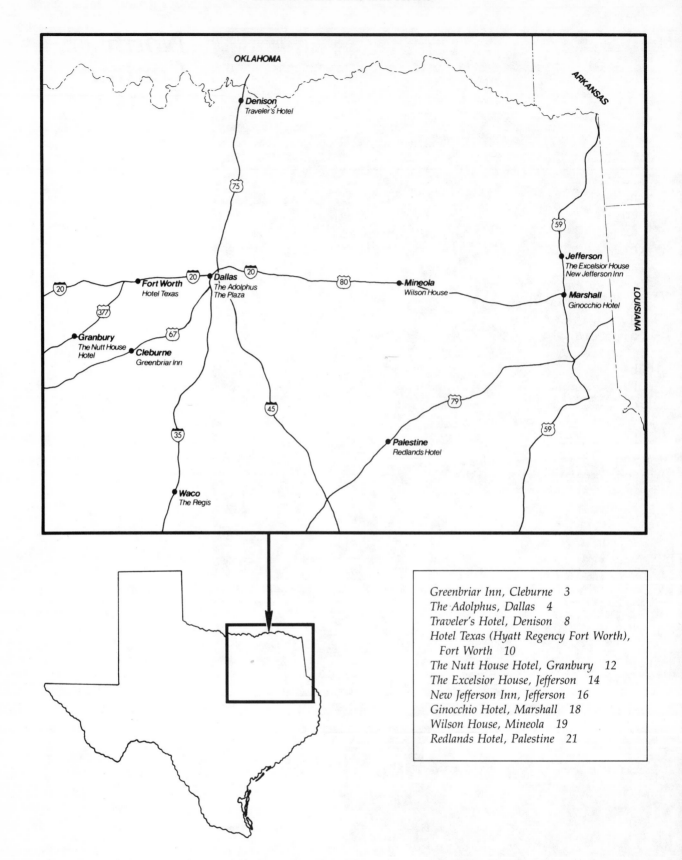

On December 14, 1924, the *Cleburne Morning Review* heralded the opening of the Liberty Hotel as "Cleburne's Fulfillment of a Long Cherished Ambition." It was "grandeur exemplified!" The article went on to rave about the magnificent furnishings, the lighting fixtures, the terrazzo floors, the modern kitchen, the elegant dining room and banquet hall, and the complete coffee shop.

A detailed description of the most expensive rooms was: "All will be equipped with baths. Heavy Wilton rugs will adorn each floor. Furnishings are bed, chiffonier, desk, table, grip stand, two fine upholstered chairs, one straight and one rocker, and windows properly draped." The reporter went on to stress that the most important feature of the bedrooms would be "a Sanidown, non-tuffed mattress, together with pure goose feather pillows." All this "grandeur" and the structure cost the princely fortune of $200,000.

It is impossible to write about this old hotel without writing about Mrs. Nell Roper. This delightful 90+ year old lady has lived in the hotel for 50 years. Imagine! Half a century of momentous occasions occurring right at your doorstep—and she remembers them all.

Mr. and Mrs. Roper moved to the Liberty Hotel when it was in its heyday. It was even built on the site of Mr. Roper's old family home. He worked for the railroad and was often on night duty. Mrs. Roper decided she would feel more comfortable about staying alone if she were in the midst of other people, and she has been here ever since. Mrs. Roper remembers when dances, banquets, and receptions were once a way of life in the grand ballroom. The restaurant would serve six or seven different meats and employed one cook to do nothing but bake breads. People came from Fort Worth and Dallas just to dine at the Liberty restaurant, and the hotel was indeed the pride of Cleburne's citizens.

Mrs. Roper also remembers the Hotsy-Totsy band led by a young man, with an unusual accent, named Lawrence Welk. And one event she will never forget is going fishing one afternoon and recognizing

Greenbriar Inn

100 E. James
Cleburne, Texas 76031
Phone: 817-645-2477
Accommodations: 54 rooms, 30
  with private bath
Rates: $20

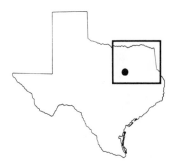

Greenbriar Inn

a famous couple in a car parked on the opposite bank—Bonnie Parker and Clyde Barrow had arrived in Cleburne. The Liberty Hotel then became the headquarters of the Texas Rangers until the infamous pair was killed a few days later in Gibsland, Louisiana, in May 1934.

The old Liberty has had different owners and now a different name, and hard times have fallen on the Greenbriar Inn. In this day and age it is a minor miracle it has survived at all. The rooms are clean, air-conditioned, and have TV, but are completely barren of any sort of decorative touch. The ballroom and restaurant are closed off completely, and the lobby that was once described as being "as attractive as may be found in any hotel of the state" is quite shabby. Signs of "No personal checks," and "Limit phone calls to 10 minutes," make it extremely difficult to envision the social events that live only in Mrs. Roper's memory.

The story of the Greenbriar Inn (the old Liberty Hotel) is the same as that of so many hotels built in this era. What was once the most important landmark in a town and the center of its social life and business activity becomes a relic and oftentimes an eyesore. The Turner Hotel in Gainsville, built in 1928, has survived as a retirement home, as has Greenville's Cadillac Hotel, built in 1926, and the Pioneer, built the same year, in Lubbock. Following the fire that wiped out a large portion of Paris, the Gibralta Hotel was erected in 1912. Of its 200 rooms, only half are usable now, and only a few floors are open. The Gibralta has become predominantly a retirement hotel. Still open, but barely, is the grand old Grim Hotel in Texarkana. Built at a cost of $1 million back in 1925, its 250 rooms made it the largest and best hotel in East Texas. Raveled and tarnished, she, too, caters to senior citizens.

As with the Greenbriar Inn (Liberty Hotel), the glorious past of these hotels is difficult to imagine today. It is somewhat astounding that they are still renting rooms when so many other hotels are standing empty. Memories of their former grandeur exist only in the minds of the older generation, as with Mrs. Nell Roper. When this generation is gone, all that will be left will be dry words in ancient newspaper clippings.

———⟨ℸ⟩———

The Adolphus

1321 Commerce
Dallas, Texas 75202
Phone: 214-742-8200
           800-227-4700
Accommodations: 435 rooms
Rates: $100 +

The Beautiful Lady with a Past. This brief phrase is a masterpiece of understatement. Not only is The Adolphus the lovliest lady in the land, her past is what novels and movie scripts are made of. When she was built in 1912, The Adolphus was "the most beautiful building west of Venice, Italy." Today the claim still holds true, for she has been restored to an elegance far surpassing her original greatness.

It is difficult to believe that all this opulence and tradition began with a lowly bottle of beer, but that is how it happened. Texas was the first state into which Adolphus Busch shipped his famous beer in the new, refrigerated cars. Overwhelmed with the response his beer received, he was determined to repay Dallas and Texas for this warm reception. Busch decided on a showplace of splendor—a hotel like none other in Texas or the United States.

Adolphus Busch was the product of an age when wealth did not have to justify its existence. He could build whatever he pleased without having to answer to anyone, which is exactly what he did. The result was 21 stories of red brick and gray granite adorned with ornate figures out of Greek mythology and capped with a tower in the shape of a beer bottle. The entire edifice was in French Renaissance style with Louis XIV wrought-iron grillwork, intricate detail in marble trim, elaborate chandeliers, and art masterpieces.

In 1904 Busch had commissioned a pair of chandeliers for exhibition at the World's Fair in St. Louis. They were encircled with eagles, the Busch company's trademark. Until The Adolphus, the two chandeliers hung in the barn housing his famous Clydesdales. With the advent of The Adolphus, one was given a place of honor in the lobby, and the other went to the St. Louis Museum. Fortunately, these magnificent pieces of art are still intact, and one is hanging above the escalator serving the registration area.

This chandelier is just one of the many treasures found in The Adolphus. More than 200 antiques and *objets d'art* like those in the

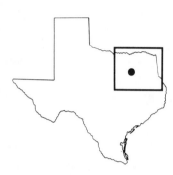

Diversions:

Six Flags Over Texas
Dallas Zoo
John F. Kennedy Memorial
State Fair Park

Louvre in Paris, in the Metropolitan Museum in New York, and in the great estates of France and England furnish the entire hotel. More than $45 million have gone into making The Adolphus the most luxurious hotel in the Old World European style. An English Regency oak table for the registration lobby is similar to one in the Louvre. Above it is a bronze Doré crystal chandelier, French, circa 1805. In the main lobby, beneath a huge skylight, are two 12 × 10 foot Brussels tapestries, dated 1661, with the town mark. Beneath the tapestries is a 19th Century English console, intricately carved, with marquetry top. Along with restored paintings from the original Adolphus, there is a large collection of extremely valuable paintings including a six-foot 19th Century French portrait of Napoleon Bonaparte. Volumes could be written just on the art treasures of The Adolphus.

The baroque hotel's renaissance includes the addition of three restaurants. Off the main lobby is The Grille, serving breakfast, lunch, and dinner in classical English style. Wing chairs, old European portraits, mahogany paneling, maps, and coats of arms create the mood of a London club. The Palm Bar has the atmosphere of a stylish New York bar. Walls are covered in burgundy wool, and the bar is burgundy marble and oak. Open weekdays only, the menu offers soups, salads, quiches, and unusual sandwiches.

But the *pièce de résistance* is the French Room. Adolphus Busch considered this room his finest jewel when the hotel opened in 1912. It has been faithfully restored in the manner of 18th Century European palaces and chateaux. Scenic designer James L. Frazer has created murals on the vaulted ceiling of cherubs holding flower garlands floating among fleecy clouds while bucolic lovers gaze soulfully into each other's eyes. The original bas-reliefs (including flowering hops) of the eight marbelized columns have been restored, and a carpet was specially handmade in Hong Kong in 59 colors. The hand-blown glass chandeliers of 17th Century design were made in Murano, Italy, by the same factory that made similar chandeliers 300 years ago. For his reservation book, the mâitre d'hôtel uses a rare Louis XV architect's table from Paris, circa 1880.

Among the more than 50 menu choices are such delicacies as Beluga caviar, royal squab salad with truffles, lobster sausage with sea urchins, sautéed pigeon garnished with liver and garlic mousse, and braised turbot with oysters and leeks. King Louis XV and his enamorata the Comtesse du Barry would believe they had never left Versailles.

The huge ceiling of the grand ballroom is also painted with clouds and rococo forms including musical instruments. As in the French Room, some of the painting was done by artists lying on their backs atop scaffolding, as Michelangelo did in the Sistine Chapel. Considered the most magnificent banquet room in the country, countless famous speakers from William Jennings Bryan to Charles Lindbergh have received applause from their admiring audiences here.

The Adolphus has also introduced the fashionable afternoon ritual of High Tea in the main lobby. Cherished in grand European hotels, High Tea offers the world's famous teas, cappuccinos, old ports and sherries, finger sandwiches, and petit fours—all on the finest service. While tea is served, a pianist plays appropriate background music.

The more than 800 guest rooms have been combined to form 439, making them the largest rooms in Dallas. All guest rooms have Williamsburg paneling and custom-made Chippendale and Queen Anne style furniture. Some of the 18 luxurious suites have outdoor terraces, and others have rooftop skylights.

The exterior of the Adolphus' original tower was not changed, only cleaned and the ornate iron grillwork restored. However, the 1917 and 1926 additions have been given a new facade with a terrace effect to draw more attention to the main tower.

High Tea is served in the after-noon in the Adolphus' walnut-paneled main lobby, which is fur-nished with one of the finest collections of art and antiques of any hotel in America.

The hotel has been host to an endless list of notables, including Presidents Franklin Roosevelt, Harry Truman, and Lyndon B. Johnson. All the big bands were here: the Dorseys, Harry James, Benny Goodman, Bob Crosby and his Bobcats, and Joe Reichman, who was adopted as Dallas' own. Then there were Hildegarde, Sophie Tucker, Joe E. Lewis, and Eddie Cantor. When radio ruled the airwaves, live broadcasts beamed throughout the Southwest from The Adolphus. It was *the* place to be on the annual Texas-Oklahoma football weekend.

The "new" Adolphus is now truly one of the most gorgeous hotels in the world. She is no doubt a "Beautiful Lady with a Past," but she is also a magnificent "Beautiful Lady with a Future."

Traveler's Hotel

*300 East Main Street
Denison, Texas 75020
Phone: 214-465-2372
Accommodations: Restaurant
   only
Hosts: Bob and Betty Brandt*

When Ernest Martin Kohl built his home in 1893, he intended for it to stand forever. The stone walls are two feet thick to withstand the vibrations of passing trains—and there were a lot of trains passing in those days: the Missouri Pacific, the Texas and Pacific, the Southern Pacific, the Frisco, the Cotton Belt Route, and the M-K-T. The M-K-T still has its offices in the grand old station, and Denison was even named for an M-K-T official, Vice President George Denison. You might just say Denison was a railroad town.

In 1906, when Kohl added the upper floor to his house, the walls were lined with galvanized metal, and ten inches of sand was laid between the floors for fire protection. The imbricated metal roof with its stamped pattern provided additional fire proofing. From a cupola on the roof, which no longer exists, Kohl raised and lowered the American flag every day.

Kohl, a former sea captain in Germany, arrived in Denison in 1855 and became successful in the grocery business. His home was a monument to his achievements. Throughout the entire house are touches of elegance. Yellow pine paneling with egg and dart trim was all hand finished and lines most of the rooms. His wine cellar was always well stocked, and it is now used as one of the restaurant's most charming dining rooms.

Kohl began taking in guests and called the house the Hotel Traveler's Home. It operated as a hotel until 1940. Purchased and lovingly restored by the Brandt brothers of Denison, it was placed on the National Register of Historic Places and opened as a restaurant in 1977.

Now, the Brandts are literally "on top of their business." They have converted the fourth floor into comfortable living quarters and have made the Traveler's Hotel Restaurant into a 24-hour-a-day job. The second floor has dining rooms for small private parties, and the third floor became the restaurant's office and additional family rooms. There are no plans to restore the building to function as a hotel.

The restaurant is a gem of restoration. Displayed above the hostess desk in the foyer are fixtures, stove, tools, etc. that were found in the house. An old metal icebox, antique shelving and back bar, ceiling fans, and the yellow pine paneling create a fine setting for the main dining room. Huge heads of moose, deer, and even eland adorn the walls—it seems a friend needed a big space to hang his trophies. The buggy shed was walled in and became part of the

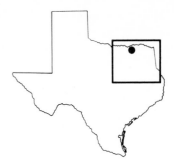

Diversons:

Lake Texoma
Dwight D. Eisenhower's
  birthplace

Traveler's Hotel

dining area, and in the old wine cellar you can still read the names on the bricks signed by members of the Kohl family.

The menu is large and quite varied. It offers seafood, steaks, Mexican food, continental specialties, salads, and sandwiches. There is a noon buffet and a chef's special from 5:30 p.m. to 10:00 p.m. The wine list is impressive, but bar drinks are by membership only, and a temporary membership can be obtained for a very nominal fee. Prices at the Traveler's Hotel are moderate, and no reservations are necessary.

Hardly anyone comes to Denison by train anymore, but the next time you drive through, head for the old M-K-T train station. "For the finest in dining," the Traveler's Hotel is right across the street.

Hotel Texas (Hyatt Regency Fort Worth)

815 Main Street
Fort Worth, Texas 76102
Phone: 817-870-1234
Accommodations: 530 rooms
Rates: $100+

Fort Worth began as a frontier army post back in 1849 and was named for General William Jenkins Worth, a Mexican War hero who never lived to see the fort named in his honor. During the era of the great cattle drives, Fort Worth's main street was a branch of the famed Chisholm Trail, so naturally the town evolved into one of the major hubs of the cattle industry.

One of these early cattle barons was Winfield Scott, who planned a luxury hotel for the city that had made him wealthy. However, Scott died in 1911 before his dream could be realized. A few years later, in 1917, the discovery of oil in the little town of Ranger 80 miles to the west changed Fort Worth forever. The city grew by the proverbial leaps and bounds, and with all this affluence came a desperate need for a first-class hotel.

By 1919 an organization known as the Citizens Hotel Company was formed, and was led by prominent businessmen. They contributed $1.2 million themselves, and almost 800 Fort Worth citizens invested another $1.8 million to finance the new hotel. It was planned to name it The Winfield in honor of the man who conceived the idea, but pride in their state led the investors to change it to Hotel Texas. When Hotel Texas opened in 1921, it was known as the "Home of the Cattle Barons," but there were a lot of those Ranger field oil barons involved in its conception, too.

Hotel Texas became the center of Fort Worth's business and social world, and the Crystal Ballroom was in constant demand. In 1926, to celebrate Texas' 100-year independence from Mexico, the city hired famed Broadway promoter Billy Rose to stage the Frontier Centennial, an incredible entertainment spectacular which would attract thousands of visitors. He held auditions in the Crystal Ballroom and turned down an aspiring young actress from nearby Weatherford. Time would prove him wrong, and Mary Martin would become a superstar without Rose's help. Many famous people came to the Hotel Texas, and it was here that John F. Kennedy spent his last night, on November 21, 1963, before that fateful day in Dallas.

In 1978 Hotel Texas became Hyatt Regency Fort Worth. Placed on the National Register of Historic Places, the red brick facade with its terra cotta steer heads will be perserved forever. However, the hotel was gutted and the world of Hyatt Regency constructed in its place. The only original feature left in the entire hotel is the ornate brass mailbox in the lobby.

The old cattle barons would gape in awe at their Hotel Texas today and probably think they had been transported to some distant world in the future. The interior is absolutely overwhelming. A 26-foot waterfall gently flows to a series of reflecting pools in the center of the lobby. Twinkling tivoli lighting, glass panels etched with modernistic cacti, and an atrium with a six-story sloping skylight create a setting right out of Tomorrowland.

Hyatt prides itself on the use of more than 730 custom-cut Texas granite pieces to form the sculptured walls, flooring, and steps in the interior. It also takes pride in some really magnificent contemporary art and sculpture displayed throughout the hotel. The centerpiece of the atrium is a geode sculpture by John Reistetter of Los Angeles, California. Rising 24 feet, it captivates the space with its starburst shape and use of brass, bronze, amethyst, and gem-quality crystals. In each guestroom are original lithographs also done by California artists. In the Cafe Centennial, a casual restaurant named for the 1936 Texas Centennial, is a patchwork tapestry

Hyatt Regency - Ft. Worth
"Hotel Texas"

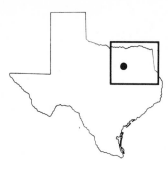

Diversions:

Amon G. Carter Museum of
*   Western Art*
Kimball Art Museum
Stockyards area
Six Flags Over Texas
Japanese Garden

featuring seven Texas stars and covering a 39-foot expanse above a seating area. Other works of patchwork art are on the lobby walls, and they, too, are the work of a California artist.

The Crystal Cactus is their fine specialty restaurant and major cocktail lounge. The central focus of the bar is provided by the use of fossilized cactus spines. Its windows are enhanced by wrought-iron gaslights. The Crystal Ballroom features a ceiling entirely covered by 27 brass and acrylic chandeliers, giving the effect of a "sea of crystal." Brass strips separating the wall panels in the Grand Crystal Ballroom complement the brass bases of the ceiling chandeliers.

The hotel guest rooms begin on the fourth level and are spacious and comfortable. Rooms are furnished in the color themes of burgundy or teal blue, with either two double beds or one king-size bed. The most prestigious accommodations are atop the hotel. The fourteenth floor houses the Regency Club with its concierge, lounge area, and complimentary hors d'oeuvres, and the fifteenth floor has its own distinctive suites offering the ultimate in luxury.

Hyatt Regency Fort Worth's goal was "to provide an experience found in no other hotel. The building's historical significance and its exquisite new interior design successfully blend yesterday and tomorrow to the benefit of guests at the Hyatt Regency Fort Worth today."

The Nutt House Hotel

Town Square
Granbury, Texas 76048
Phone: 817-573-5612
Accommodations: 8 guest
*   rooms, 3 baths*
Rates: $12–$33
Innkeeper: Mary Lou Watkins

So much has been written about Granbury—its citizens, its restoration, its opera house, its courthouse, its charm and appeal—that most superlatives are repetitious. The entire town square has been placed on the National Register of Historic Places and has won many other civic awards, including the prestigious Lester Award for contributions in historic preservation.

The minute you arrive in Granbury you are aware of how different it is from so many small Texas towns. Instead of the usual deserted stores, dilapidated movie theatre, and often seedy courthouse, Granbury is positively vibrant with activity and exudes an aura of prosperity. The Opera House is a tremendous drawing card, for the performances are very professional, and tickets are often difficult to come by. But a great deal of Granbury's success in becoming a major tourist attraction rather than a neglected and bankrupt small town goes to a dynamic woman named Mary Lou Watkins. This great-granddaughter of the town's first Nutts has inspired Granbury to become a true Texas treasure.

The town's revival started with Mary Lou opening The Nutt House Restaurant on the portentous day (if you believe in omens) of April 1, 1970. This lady and her new venture were a success from the start. Now The Nutt House is renowned all over Texas as one of its best restaurants. There is no menu, and the table is set "as moth-

The Nutt House

ers and grandmothers did at the turn of the century." The regional fare includes such favorites as chicken and dumplings, meat loaf, ham, and always four vegetables in season. Best of all, you also get Mary Lou's superb hot-water cornbread. For a pittance you can purchase a sack of cornbread mix with her famous recipe at The Nutt House Gift Shop. The restaurant is open every day at noon except Mondays, but supper is served only on Thursday and Friday.

The Nutt House was erected for two blind brothers, Jesse and Jacob Nutt, in 1893. The building was originally a grocery store, but was later converted into The Nutt Hotel about 1919. This hand-hewn stone building has been occupied by three generations of the Nutt family. Once again functioning as a hotel, the guest rooms are just delightful. The single rooms are still quite small, but some walls have been knocked out, and the doubles are spacious. All are furnished as if the year were still 1919, and even though they have screen doors and ceiling fans, the hotel is centrally air-conditioned. The upstairs parlor is a bonanza of old ledgers and registers that make wonderful browsing. There is also an apartment with a sitting room, a bedroom with a double bed, a kitchen-dining area, and a bath—an ideal place for a family gathering or small party.

In the small lobby, which is also the entrance to the restaurant, be sure to look at Mary Lou's scrapbook with all the many clippings and articles written about Granbury and The Nutt House. Every major magazine has lauded this little town that has so beautifully retained its Texas heritage. Thanks to dedicated people such as Mary Lou Watkins, we can share Granbury's past today.

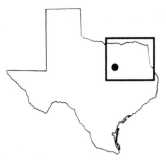

Diversions:

Granbury Opera House
Lake Granbury
Granbury Historical Courthouse
  Square
Dinosaur State Park, Glen Rose

The Excelsior House

Jefferson, Texas 75657
Phone: 214-665-2513
Accommodations: 12 with bath,
* 2 share bath, 1 suite*
Rates: $10 - $25, suite $40
Innkeeper: Cissy McCampbell

Today towns die because the interstate highways bypass them, but in the 1800s towns died when the railroad bypassed them. In 1882 Jay Gould, the railroad magnate, signed the guest register of The Excelsior House with "End of Jefferson, Texas."

Gould wanted the town to give him the right-of-way for his Texas and Pacific line, but Jefferson wanted Gould to purchase the land. Neither side gave in, and it seemed for a while that Gould's dire prediction would come true.

Jefferson had been one of the major cities in Texas during the steamboat era, and The Excelsior House hosted such notables as Ulysses S. Grant, Rutherford B. Hayes, Oscar Wilde, Jacob Astor, and W.H. Vanderbilt. However, with the end of the steamboat and the absence of a railroad, Jefferson turned from a predominant river port bustling with commerce to a sleepy country town. Yet the hotel, then called the Irvine House, has managed to stay in business since the 1850s. The Historical Society is not sure when or how the name was changed to The Excelsior House, but the following verse from Longfellow's *Excelsior* was quoted on their brochure for years:

> A traveller, by the faithful hound,
> Half-buried in the snow was found,
> Still grasping in his hand of ice
> That banner with the strange device,
>   *Excelsior!*

The Excelsior House

In 1961 The Excelsior House was up for sale, and a dedicated group of women managed to raise the $30,000 needed to buy it. Since that time the Jesse Allen Wise Garden Club has owned and operated the hotel. Their foresight and vision have paid off handsomely, for The Excelsior House is booked continuously, and reservations must be made as far in advance as possible. Restoration and refurbishing were made possible by the donations of wonderful people who loved the old place, and craftsmen gave their time and skills to bring the hotel back to its original elegance.

Today, a visit to The Excelsior House is a very special event. As you look at the rooms all done in gorgeous cherry, maple, and mahogany antiques, it is overwhelming to realize the amount of time, money, and thought that went into the restoration. There are Oriental carpets on polished floors, swagged drapries on the windows, and portraits on the walls.

Some of the rooms are named. The Lady Bird Room was refurbished in honor of the First Lady by some of her East Texas friends. Jefferson has even forgiven the man who predicted her doom—hence the Jay Gould Room. The Presidential Suite has an enormous 4-poster with a 10-foot canopy, red walls, and a fantastic bathroom. Have you ever slept in a sleigh? You can at The Excelsior House, as the gorgeous old bed in the Sleigh Bed Bedroom is built to resemble one. Even the rooms that aren't named are all decorated in period furniture. If you are unable to stay at The Excelsior House, all the rooms are open during certain times each day for a small fee.

Another real highlight of The Excelsior House is breakfast. It is the only meal served, and one of the best treats in Texas. For about $3.50 you can savor a plantation breakfast of ham, grits, eggs, and Cissy's world-renowed Orange Blossom muffins. You dine in the lovely garden room that looks out into the patio. If there is an extra-large crowd, you may be seated at the gleaming mahogany 20-place table in the dining room with its magnificent French brass and porcelain chandelier. You do not have to be a hotel guest to make a reservation for this delicious breakfast.

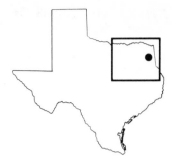

Diversions:

Jay Gould Railroad Car,
  Atalanta
Jefferson Historical Museum
Freeman Plantation
The entire historical district of
  Jefferson

The Grant Room, beautifully restored and maintained by the Jesse Allen Wise Garden Club.

The hotel ballroom recalls the splendor of the steamboat era.

The hotel ballroom with its pressed-tin ceiling, oriental rugs, grand piano, and crystal chandelier makes a most impressive place for parties and receptions at a very reasonable fee.

The Excelsior House is what memories are made of. Heaven only knows what stories those walls and floors could tell. Not only is this the most romantic hotel in Texas, it has been open for guests longer than any other. If all those famous, and even those not so famous, guests were to return, they would all feel right at home and never notice the years that have passed. You have the feeling The Excelsior House has always been this way and will endure forever.

New Jefferson Inn

124 West Austin Street
Jefferson, Texas 75657
Phone: 214-665-2361
Accommodations: 22 rooms, all
with bath
Rates: $20 +
Innkeepers: Mr. and Mrs.
George Delk

Back in the 1850s and 1860s, Jefferson was one of the most important seaports in Texas. It rivaled Galveston in exporting Texas farm products, lumber, and iron ore, and in importing goods from all over the world. People were not aware that this waterway into the Red River was an unnatural situation. They had no way of knowing that when the Army Corps of Engineers cleared the debris from the main channel the water level would drop drastically. So until 1874, when this happened, Jefferson was one of the busiest and richest towns in Texas. Jefferson was so secure in her river trade she refused to grant money or land to Jay Gould to bring his railroad to the town. The railroad went to Marshall instead, and by the turn of the century riverboats had been replaced by the iron horse. Jefferson, "The Gateway to Texas," was dying.

In 1861 a huge warehouse was built to store the numerous cotton bales awaiting shipment down the river. By 1900 when there were no more riverboats and no need for warehouses, the old building

New Jefferson Inn

was converted into a hotel. In 1977 the Delks restored and revitalized the old warehouse-hotel into a charming hostelry, the New Jefferson Inn.

The well-appointed lobby contains lovely marble-top tables, antique sofas and chairs, an old hotel desk, and a key box. In the upstairs hallway are some really beautiful old pieces of furniture. The guest rooms on the second floor are all quite large and decorated with turn-of-the-century iron beds, Victorian dressers, rocking chairs, and straight chairs. The queen-size beds are reproductions, but the accessory pieces are all vintage. A few of the baths have claw-footed tubs, but for the most part the fixtures are all modern. All rooms come with air-conditioning units, TV, and some with ceiling fans.

The dining room is tastefully decorated with mirrors and paintings and open for breakfast and lunch Tuesday through Saturdays. Dinner is served Friday and Saturday only. The menu includes a full "plantation" breakfast and luncheon specials such as Swiss steak, roast beef, and baked ham. The weekend dinners offer several steaks and a wide selection of seafood.

Old-fashioned benches in front of the New Jefferson Inn provide a delightful spot to enjoy the serenity of Jefferson today. In the evenings, only occasional passing cars down the old brick streets disturb the peace and quiet of this marvelous little town. About the only entertainment at night is to stroll around and read the historical markers. Nearly every building has one, for there are 59 on various homes, churches, and businesses. But you don't come to Jefferson for excitement. You come for a trip back in time to antebellum Texas. With the restoration of so many fine buildings, tourists have brought prosperity back to Jefferson, but she still maintains her leisurely pace and wonderful Texas hospitality.

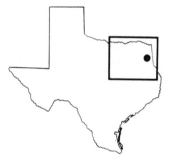

Diversions:

Lake O'the Pines
Jay Gould's Railroad Car
  Atalanta
Jefferson Historical Museum
Old Homes Tour

Ginocchio Hotel

701 N. Washington
Marshall, Texas 75670
Phone: 214-938-8491
Accommodations: Restaurant
  only

Ghosts, graves, and tunnels: The Ginocchio Hotel likes to think it has them all, and it is certainly old enough to qualify for all three. Built in 1896 by Charles Ginocchio, a Greek immigrant, it was the finest hotel between New Orleans and Denver. Twenty-six passenger trains a day came through Marshall, and it was nothing for the Ginocchio Hotel to serve more than 400 meals daily. Passengers used the tunnel under the tracks to get from the station to the hotel.

There is a theory that another tunnel exists in the basement of the hotel, and a sealed entrance down there defies explanation. Some say the mystery tunnel went under the street to Ginocchio's home where he stored his fine wines to keep them from being pilfered in the hotel bar. Others say it was used during Prohibition to smuggle "shine." And some say there is no tunnel at all, as the Ginocchio home has no entrance for one.

Nor is there any explanation for the mystery of the trap door in the floor of the hotel dining room. One rather romantic theory is that someone could drop through the trap door into the basement and escape via the tunnel for a fast getaway.

Another unexplained puzzle is the hole 2.5 × 6 feet dug in the basement floor where once was solid concrete. This grave-size hole has been chipped out and packed with dirt for no apparent reason. It certainly was not used to work on the plumbing, for the pipes all hang from the ceiling.

As for the resident ghost, no one has actually seen it, but there are various reports of hearing it walking about. A medium said it was a female spirit that was very friendly and lived in the gargoyle over the mirror. As far as anyone knows, she is still there and still friendly.

The Ginocchio doesn't need things that go bump in the night to be a fantastic old building. The curly pine paneling throughout the hotel and on the stairway is a masterpiece of workmanship and design. Ginocchio admired this particular pine that was being used in the Texas and Pacific shops by Pullman for parlor cars. So he bought an entire stand of pine to be used in his hotel. The wood was so

Ginocchio Hotel

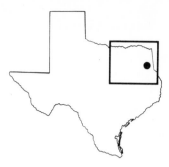

difficult to machine that much of the finishing had to be done by hand. When it was restored, it took over 800 gallons of paint remover to remove generations of dark finish, oil, soot, and dirt. A disease in the pine had given it the "curly" effect, and when the trees grew back, they were no longer diseased. Therefore the woodwork in the hotel can never be duplicated.

The grand staircase has long been used by brides for throwing their bouquets, and it also hides a secret weapon. The ball of the newel post comes out with a handle, making it a formidable club. To the right of the second floor landing is the Murphy Stoop. No one knows why it is called by this name, but this pie-shaped balcony was a perfect spot for the manager to keep an eye on the lobby and the staircase as well.

The elk head in the upstairs bar is said to be the largest to come out of the Oklahoma Territory. Stored in the attic for years, when it was rediscovered it was practically a bald elk. Glue and contributions from the Ginocchio barbershop have restored it to its regal majesty.

The arches in the lobby sport the first electric lights sold by the Edison Electric Light Company in the Southwest. Supplied by wet-cell batteries in the bottom of the center column, they were turned on for visiting dignitaries and Presidents Taft, Harding, and Wilson. Just in case the new-fangled invention didn't work, gas lights were installed, too.

All of these treasures are still here, and so much more. You can get a shoeshine from the old hotel shoeshine stand, ice cream from the antique soda fountain, or popcorn from the original popcorn machine. The lobby has been restored as a reception room for the restaurant. The restaurant offers a daily special, sandwiches, and salads for lunch, and a marinated steak in garlic sauce as the dinner specialty.

The upstairs sitting room is now a bar and lounge and serves a wide variety of delicious hors d'oeuvres. Down the hall from the bar, 12 rooms are being restored for guests. Visitors may not arrive by train anymore, and there is some ugly talk of tearing down the wonderful old train station; but when guests come to the Ginocchio Hotel, they will enter the Victorian Era in Texas at its best.

Diversions:

*Marshall Pottery Factory and
    Old World Store*
Marshall Historical District
Lake O'the Pines

Even though Mineola has a rather Indian sound to its name, it is just another railroad town. Ira Evans, a railroad man, named the station in honor of his daughter, Ola, and his daughter's friend, Minnie Patton. When the trains quit running, Mineola became just another little East Texas town with not much going for it.

As Mineola owed its origin to the railroad, so did the "Old Bailey Hotel." This impressive old brick structure was completed by Michael Augustus Bailey in 1913. Its more than 50 rooms housed

Wilson House

111 Front Street
Mineola, Texas 75773
Phone: 214-569-3922
*Accommodations: Restaurant
    only*
Hosts: Vi and Sam Wilson

drummers and travelers on the thriving railroad, for back in those days Mineola was a major transfer point. In 1940 Bailey's heirs sold the hotel to Carlton B. Jones, and it then became the Carlton Hotel. Mr. Jones lived there until his death in 1975, and in the spring of 1976 it became the Wilson House.

The Wilsons came to Mineola and the Old Bailey because, as Vi, the owner, put it, "It was the only place I could find big enough for my antiques." Neither the Old Bailey nor the Carlton ever had the furnishings as Wilson House does now. The Wilsons have made a veritable showcase of the downstairs, and some of their antiques are worthy of any museum. Particularly impressive is a massive desk in the center of the lobby, but don't miss any of the other antiques, for they are all gorgeous. One of the original public rooms is now a private dining room with a magnificent table and chairs and stained glass windows. It makes a perfect setting for a special private party.

The floors in the lobby and dining room are narrow-cut oak and maple hardwood. Walls are plaster with five-foot wooden wainscoting. The 12-foot tin ceilings are pressed in a sculptured design, and the front doors are beveled glass flanked by large plate-glass windows.

The old dining room is now one of the most gracious restaurants in East Texas. Oriental antiques, lace curtains, candlelight, china plates, and waitresses in long skirts create a very refined atmosphere. Absolutely superb food consists of a choice of a meat, fish or chicken entrée, with the rest of the menu the chef's choice. A typical dinner begins with tiny cheese puffs and tuna and jalepeño appetizers. Next is a green salad with the house dressing, then a chicken and rice soup. The entrée is served with mixed vegetables, and with it comes homemade Parker House rolls. Dessert of fresh

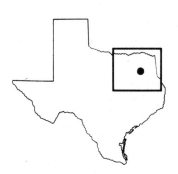

Diversions:

Tyler Rose Garden, Tyler

Wilson House

fruit, cake, and Wilson House ice cream is all served buffet style with as many helpings as you wish of each. To complete the whole elegant picture, seated at the grand piano in the lobby is a lovely little lady in an organdy evening dress playing just the right music to set the tone of the evening.

Wilson House is only open on Saturday nights, and reservations are a must. If you can't reach the Wilsons by phone, just drop them a note stating when you want to come to dinner. Alcoholic beverages are not served, but it is perfectly *à propos* to bring your own wine or whatever you prefer. Set-ups are provided.

Mineola is hardly the place you would choose for an exciting weekend, but it is the perfect choice for a memorable dining experience. Vi summed up the whole evening quite succinctly with, "We really do have lovely guests at Wilson House."

Redlands Hotel

400 N. Queen Street
Palestine, Texas 75801
Phone: 214-723-1444
Accommodations: Restaurant
  only
Hosts: Robert and Jean Laughlin

The Redlands Hotel is another of many an old derelict that had its brief glory during the railroad era. Palestine (the locals are quick to correct you that the town is pronunced Palesteen) is still a big railroad town, but without the passengers so necessary for a hotel's "reason to be." Opening in 1915, the Redlands was then one of the finest hotels in the state. It was built at a cost of $100,000 by the Palestine Hotel Company, composed of local citizens and financial institutions. It was considered extremely modern in every detail, because its 86 rooms all had telephones, lavatories, hot and cold water, and many had private baths.

A March 21, 1915, article in the *Galveston News* described the hotel and the lobby as "commodious with a large ceiling skylight and

The Redlands

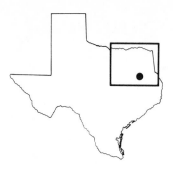

Diversions:

Texas State Railroad with restored Victorian depots at Palestine and Rusk

large and inviting doors at the main and side entrances." The article went on to report the formal banquet at the opening, but most of the details were quotes of toasts from the attending dignitaries. For such an auspicious occasion, the toasts were rather bland. A representative of the International and great Northern Railroad said, "The People and the Railroads." The mayor of Palestine, A. L. Bowers, very simply stated, "Our city." And the proprietor of the Redlands, E. W. Shubert, came up with, "Why I came to Palestine."

Shubert did not have a long stay in the city of his choice, for the Redlands only lasted a brief four years and closed its doors in 1919. Reasons for its failure are lost in the past, but it is strange that it should be unprofitable when the twenties would see a massive boom in hotel construction. The hotel was then leased to the International and Great Northern Railroad and used as their general offices until 1956.

For nearly 20 years this grand old building stood abandoned. Finally, in 1976, it was purchased for $10,000 by Robert L. Laughlin. He and his sister, Mary Jean Laughlin, moved to Palestine and embarked on the awesome task of restoring the Redlands.

The first part of the building to re-open was an antique shop in what was once the hotel dining room. Jean's Victorian Antiques offers a variety of turn-of-the-century items, and a few other shops and businesses help maintain a lively atmosphere.

Robert Laughlin runs the Landmark, a teahouse and restaurant with Victorian decor, located in a corner of the Redlands. Gourmet foods highlight the menu along with the standard East Texas fare. Steak Diane is a dinner entrée along with chicken fried steak. Homemade egg bread, sweet bread, and fruit bread are big favorites, and you can have fresh popovers if you give the restaurant an hour's notice. Famous Landmark desserts are sour cream pie and buttermilk pie. No alcoholic beverages are sold (nor can you bring any), and prices are very reasonable.

The Redlands Hotel is one of the highlights of the Historic Palestine Downtown Walking Tour. Visitors are invited to browse and dine in what is once again one of Palestine's finest landmarks.

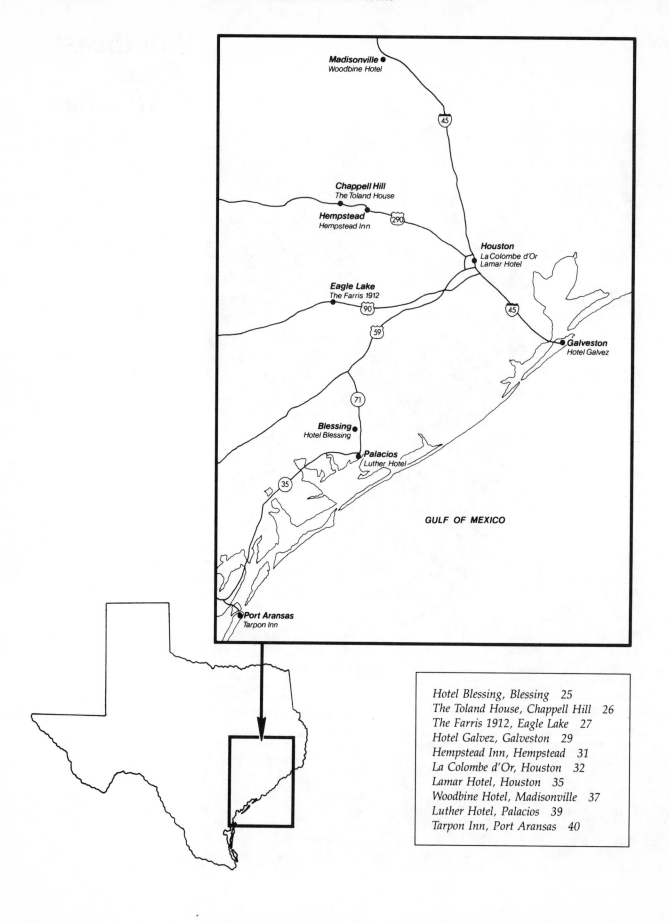

Madisonville ●
Woodbine Hotel

45

Chappell Hill
The Toland House

Hempstead
Hempstead Inn

290

Houston
La Colombe d'Or
Lamar Hotel

Eagle Lake
The Farris 1912

90

59

45

● **Galveston**
Hotel Galvez

71

Blessing ●
Hotel Blessing

Palacios ●
Luther Hotel

35

GULF OF MEXICO

● **Port Aransas**
Tarpon Inn

Hotel Blessing, Blessing 25
The Toland House, Chappell Hill 26
The Farris 1912, Eagle Lake 27
Hotel Galvez, Galveston 29
Hempstead Inn, Hempstead 31
La Colombe d'Or, Houston 32
Lamar Hotel, Houston 35
Woodbine Hotel, Madisonville 37
Luther Hotel, Palacios 39
Tarpon Inn, Port Aransas 40

Hotel Blessing

Blessing, Texas 77419
Phone: 512-588-6806
Accommodations: 25 rooms, 5
 baths
Rates: $15.00-$17.50

Back in 1902, Jonathan Edwards Pierce was so grateful the railroad finally reached his part of Texas, he wanted to name the new town "Thank God." The post office rejected that idea, so he settled for "Blessing," for the railroad was indeed a blessing. In 1906 Pierce built the Hotel Blessing out of clapboard in the Mission Style of architecture. Unlike any other hotel built during this era, it is surprising that Hotel Blessing was not the typical Victorian gingerbread so popular in those years. Instead, it rather looks like a wooden Alamo. Jonathan Pierce's grandson, A. B. Pierce, Jr., and his wife, Ruth, have now donated the hotel to the Blessing Historical Foundation, and it has been added to the National Register of Historic Places and designated a Texas Historic Landmark.

Restoration of the building has begun, but the hotel rstaurant has been offering down-home cooking with a down-home atmosphere for years. You used to go right into the kitchen and help yourself out of huge pots simmering on the stoves. Now the stoves have moved into the dining room, but the pots are still there, as delicious as ever.

Lunch is served from 11 a.m. until 2 p.m., and what a lunch it is! For $4.00 you can have all you can eat of eight different vegetables, at least three meats, four salads, two kinds of gravy, relishes, homemade corn bread and white bread, iced tea, and—if you still have room after all that—peach cobbler. Particularly delicious is the barbequed chicken, the cream gravy, and the corn bread. And everything is so good you don't mind plastic tablecloths, paper napkins, and artificial lemon juice. Helen Feldhousen, the manager, has a staff of local cooks that really know how to set a table—or, rather, how to set a stove!

Even though lunch is served buffet style, there is also an à la carte breakfast beginning at 6:00 a.m. The highest priced item on the standard breakfast menu is 3 eggs with 2 hotcakes and meat for $3.00.

Hotel Blessing

Diversions:

Matagorda Beach
Palacios Bay

The exterior of the hotel has a fresh coat of gray paint with white trim, and it looks much as it did in 1906. However, restoration of the interior has barely begun. One of the downstairs rooms has been refurbished to show what the Historical Foundation has in mind for all guest rooms. Charmingly furnished in old pieces, it also has a ceiling fan. The rooms upstairs have screened doors with plain white curtains across them, and none are air-conditioned. Sparsely furnished, they are just basic accommodations. Not much has been done to the lobby, but it does have original ceiling fans, key rack, ancient drinking fountain, and exposed pipes everywhere.

The possibilities for the Hotel Blessing are limitless, and the Historical Foundation has placed a sign in the dining room telling you how to "Be a Friend of Hotel Blessing." You can decorate a room, air-condition a room, add a bath, add a light fixture, donate a portrait of an early settler, insulate the attic, donate kitchen equipment or a longhorn steer head, or pave a parking space.

There is no way you can visit the old Hotel Blessing and not fall in love with it. Perhaps you'll love her so much *you'll* want to make a donation. It would indeed be a blessing.

The Toland House

Main at Poplar
Chappell Hill, Texas 77426
Accommodations: 4 rooms, 3 baths
Rates: $25-$30
Innkeeper: Eve Knapp

One of the smallest Texas inns is located in one of the smallest Texas towns. Good things do come in small packages, however, and The Toland House proves it.

In 1912 Mary Hale Toland, the widow of a pioneer physician, determined to build a residential hotel. The two-story frame structure was erected for her by a local contractor, "Deacon" Heartfield, at the corner of Main and Poplar Streets. Dr. Toland's small office which had previously occupied this site was moved to the rear, attached to the house, and became the new kitchen and store room. A sign,

The Toland House

simply lettered HOTEL, was nailed to the front of the building. In this little village, no further identification was required.

The Toland Hotel was an immediate success. Clean, comfortable rooms and Mrs. Toland's bountiful table assured satisfaction among the guests. It continued to operate until Mrs. Toland's death in 1931. It then became a private residence of various owners until the spring of 1980 when it was reopened in its role of country inn.

The inn has been so perfectly restored, it looks as though "Deacon" Heartfield just put the finishing touches to it. The "Honeymoon suite" on the first floor has a grandiose four-poster bed that takes up most of the room. The three upstairs rooms are not furnished in antiques, but all are very comfortable and absolutely spotless. One is referred to as "The Rooster Room," because the neighborhood rooster is guaranteed to wake you up in the morning.

There is a tiny parlor, a dining room, and a kitchen with a refrigerator that is never empty of complimentary cheese and wine. Innkeeper Eve Knapp also serves her guests a continental breakfast. This charming lady has a wonderful knack of making her guests feel really welcome at The Toland House. Naturally the inn has a front porch to sit on and watch "Chappell Hill go by."

Chappell Hill is a very old Texas town and well worth exploring. It has a small museum, a one-room library, several antique shops, and a Methodist church with interesting beaded glass windows. But you don't come to Chappell Hill for the "sights." You come to Chappell Hill because it offers a truly restful respite from "progress."

The friendly folks in Chappell Hill will be glad to have you any season, but the most beautiful time of year is in April during bluebonnet season. The rolling hills are so thick with flowers they look like vast blue lakes. It is easy to forget sometimes how many scenic wonders Texas actually has, but during the spring when the wild flowers are in bloom, the whole state offers a gorgeous view. And one of the best parts of all this beauty is at Chappell Hill.

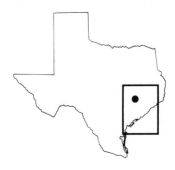

Diversions:

Bluebonnet Hills Restaurant, Highway 290 West, family-style country cooking
Washington-on-the-Brazos
Round Top

The Farris 1912

201 N. McCarty at Post Office Street
Eagle Lake, Texas 77434
Accommodations: 16 rooms, 4 baths
Rates: $36-$42 off season
$70 during season
Innkeepers: Bill and Helyn Farris

Eagle Lake has long been famous for having the best duck and goose hunting in Texas. Now with its old hotel re-opened, The Farris 1912, the town has another claim to fame. Originally named The Hotel Dallas, this hotel was erected in 1912 and considered the epitome of everything great one could expect to find in rural Texas. The Hotel Dallas was hailed as the finest small-town hotel in the state. With the depression of the 1930s, this red brick building fell into a state of pitiful disrepair.

After several years of admiring the old hotel, William and Helyn Farris purchased it in 1974. Because the hotel had always carried the name of the proprietor, and because 1912 was Eagle Lake's golden era, the Hotel was rechristened The Farris 1912. Restoration took several years, and overnight guests were finally welcomed in 1977.

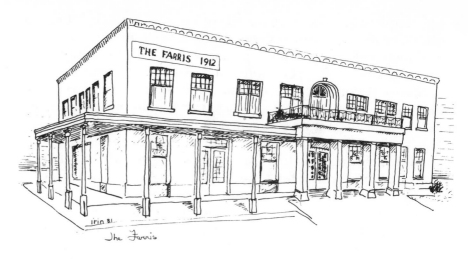

The Farris 1912 is once again a true gem of small hotels. It is difficult to think of enough superlatives to describe the furnishings and decor throughout the hotel. Lovely and unusual antiques grace every room, creating the original elegant atmosphere. No matter where you look, there is a point of interest. Parlors and public rooms are especially charming with their Victorian pieces.

The solarium on the first floor is the perfect setting for parties and receptions, and the mezzanine offers a more informal atmosphere with its ceiling fans, game table, TV and old wicker furniture. Bill Farris said, "There have been more birds killed around this [game] table than were ever shot in the blinds."

Guest rooms open off the mezzanine and each is absolutely perfect. Two have their own baths, and all have twin beds. Walls are painted in bright colors, and one particularly charming room is done in shades of Victorian purple. Towel stands were especially de-

The second-floor mezzanine is a favorite gathering place of hunters telling tall tales before dinner is served.

signed for the hotel, and there is wall-to-wall carpeting throughout. The only TV is on the mezzanine.

Before going into dinner in The Drummers Room, you may wish to look around the varied and lovely items in the hotel gift shop. Dinner is a delightful meal, with candlelight, lace tablecloths, and very good food. Helyn Farris is the chef, and she knows exactly how to please her guests. There is a fixed menu, but you do have a choice of entrées. Only wine and beer are available, but setups are furnished. The Drummers Room is open on weekends only.

During duck and goose hunting season (November, December, and January), The Farris 1912 offers only the American Plan. A room with three gourmet country-style meals and hors d'oeuvres before dinner is $70 per person. Also, extra little services are provided for hunters such as filling your thermos before you leave, having dry shoes waiting for you on your return, and meeting your plane. All of these amenities are at no extra charge, so it is easy to see why the hotel is always packed during this busy season.

The year 1912 may have begun one golden era for Eagle Lake, but William and Helyn Farris are well on the way to another golden era with this wonderful hotel. The Farris 1912 is truly "A step back in time, the Queen of early Texas hotels, with the comforts of today."

Diversions:

Northington Plantation Museum, Egypt
Attwater Prairie Chicken National Wildlife Refuge

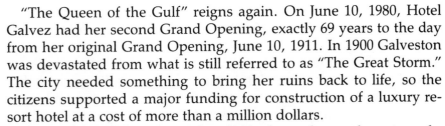

"The Queen of the Gulf" reigns again. On June 10, 1980, Hotel Galvez had her second Grand Opening, exactly 69 years to the day from her original Grand Opening, June 10, 1911. In 1900 Galveston was devastated from what is still referred to as "The Great Storm." The city needed something to bring her ruins back to life, so the citizens supported a major funding for construction of a luxury resort hotel at a cost of more than a million dollars.

When Hotel Galvez opened in 1911, above the north porte-cochere was the coat of arms of Count Bernardo de Galvez, the namesake of Galveston. It read *Yo Solo* (I Alone), a fitting tribute to the solitary determination of a city rising from the wake of the storm. A large oil portrait of the Count hung in the hotel lobby for years. Later, it belonged to Mr. and Mrs. F. Russell Kendall who had the painting restored and presented it to Archie Bennett, Jr. and Dr. Denton Cooley, owners of Marriott's Hotel Galvez. The portrait can be viewed today at the end of the west lobby.

Hotel Galvez has been host to many celebrities and world leaders. Franklin D. Roosevelt made it his temporary White House during a fishing trip. Douglas MacArthur was here, and so were Dwight D. Eisenhower and Richard M. Nixon. Alice Fay and Phil Harris, stars of the forties were married in a Galvez suite. Then there were the Dorsey brothers, Paul Whiteman, and Frank Sinatra. Many others came to perform in the hotel ballroom, while some received top bill-

Hotel Galvez

21st Street and Seawall Boulevard
Galveston, Texas 77550
Phone: 713-765-7721
Reservations: 1-800-228-9290
Accommodations: 224 rooms
Rates: $85 +

Marriott - Galvez

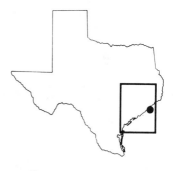

Diversions:

The Historic Strand
The Bishop's Palace
Sea-Arama Marine World
Lone Star Outdoor
   Amphitheater
Galveston-Port Bolivar Ferry
Galveston Island State Park

ing in the Balinese Room across the street. When gambling was wide open in Galveston, the Balinese Room was the most popular night spot in Texas, and her stars always had suites at the Hotel Galvez.

This Spanish-style stucco hotel has now received a $13-million renovation. Marriott felt it necessary to gut the entire interior from the second floor up and construct new Marriott-quality guest rooms. Fortunately, however, the first floor has been refurbished back to its 1911 charm. The original entrance with its handsome porte-cochere on the north side (away from the Gulf) is used once again. On the Gulf side, an indoor and an outdoor pool and an al fresco lounge have been added.

The Promenade facing the Gulf has its wicker furniture back in place, its ceiling fans, red floral carpet, beamed ceilings, and the Count Galvez family crests. Lighting fixtures have been faithfully reproduced, and also the hotel desk. Walls are hung with enlarged photographs of old Galveston in heavy gold frames, and huge potted plants are everywhere. All of this Victorian elegance makes this the ideal place to sit and watch the eternal surf break on Galveston Beach.

The dining room with its arched windows is cream and gold, as it was in 1911. Chairs are upholstered in several different patterns, which all blend perfectly. Chandeliers, brass fixtures, white tablecloths, and canopies make this by far the lovliest dining room in the city. A breakfast buffet is served daily, and the à la carte dinner menu features prime rib, steak, and seafood. Appetizers include baked oysters and nacholupas (elegant tacos). The menu is cleverly presented as a photograph album of Hotel Galvez when she first opened. Some are the same photos on the hotel walls.

Yes, the "Queen of the Gulf" is back, more beautiful than ever.

When Anne Issa designed her sign for the Hempstead Inn, she decided on a lovely lass perched in the moon, smiling a warm welcome for guests. After being complimented on the sign's originality, Anne said, "It's symbolic of starting this inn—I might as well reach for the moon." The Hempstead Inn has won not only the moon, but also the sun and the evening star as well. Success was instantaneous with the Inn's good location, nice rooms, and excellent food.

The turn-of-the-century clapboard inn was once a boarding house back when Hempstead was known as "Six-Shooter Junction." The stories go that the town was so wild and wooly, train passengers huddled on the coach floor to avoid being in the line of fire of ricocheting bullets—but you know how stories tend to get a bit distorted with time. The building is certainly old enough for a Texas Historic Landmark, but historical requirements are that buildings must be on the same site for 50 years. When the trains stopped arriving, the boarding house was moved from the railroad tracks to the highway, less than half a block. But, regardless, it was moved, so the Hempstead Inn will have to wait a few more years for its marker.

Guest rooms are fairly large, bathrooms are modern, and the inn has central heating and air-conditioning. Furnishings are eclectic with iron beds, some fairly new pieces, and some antiques. The mixture produces pleasant results, and each room has its own decor and personality. A small porch upstairs offers a secluded spot to watch the rushed world of Highway 290 whiz by.

The lobby with its nice sofa, chairs, and coffee table could be someone's living room. It is a comfortable place to wait in case there is a line of hungry patrons for the Publick Dining Room, and chances are there will be, for word about the inn's good food has spread.

The dining room itself is quite plain, with bare floors, bare windows, and painted white walls. The room does have two hand-carved breakfronts that are more than 300 years old and just magnificent.

Hempstead Inn

435 10th Street (Highway 290 N.)
Hempstead, Texas 77445
Phone: 713-826-6379
Accommodations: 8 rooms, 4 baths
Rates: $25 - $30
Innkeepers: Anne and Ghazi Issa

Hempstead Inn

Diversions:

Best vegetable and fruit markets north of Corpus Christi.

The table in the old boarding house never groaned under a load of food the way Ghazi's does now. Yet the meals are prepared much as they were back in those old times when everything had to be fresh and cornbread didn't come out of box or biscuits out of a can. Ghazi says his kitchen doesn't even have a can opener. There is no menu, nor is one necessary. You know that whatever the fare of the day is, it will be bountiful and delicious. Served family style, a typical meal might be pan-fried chicken, fried fish, meatloaf, numerous vegetables in season, mashed potatoes, (and not the dried flakes, either) rice, a fresh fruit salad made with Hempstead's famous watermelons when in season, cornbread, and biscuits. Ghazi's biscuits are the kind you could make a meal on just by themselves.

The dining room is open from 11 a.m. to 2 p.m. and from 5 p.m.–10 p.m. weekdays, and from 11 a.m. to 10 p.m. on weekends. Ghazi plans to add duck, quail, and pheasant to his repertoire, and they, too, will no doubt be a culinary treat. If you wish, you can arrange for a candlelight dinner on the upstairs balcony.

The next time you go through Hempstead, look for the sign with the damsel in the moon and treat yourself to an outstanding repast and a pleasant stay at one of Texas' newest old inns.

La Colombe d'Or

*3410 Montrose Boulevard
Houston, Texas 77006
Phone: 713-524-7999
Accommodations: 5 rooms, all
    with bath
Rates: $150–$200 per day
Innkeeper: Steve Zimmerman*

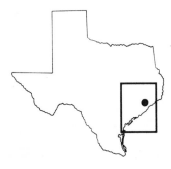

In Texas, where it is a matter of status to have everything "the biggest," Steve Zimmerman prides himself on having "the smallest." La Colombe d'Or is not only the smallest full-service luxury hotel in Texas, it is the smallest full-service luxury hotel in the United States. It is not just "luxurious," it is exquisitely and magnificently luxurious.

In Steve's travels his favorite place to go is La Colombe d'Or, an *auberge* in St. Paul de Vence, France. Translated as The Golden Dove, it is an inn with antique-filled guest rooms and a superb restaurant. It features an art collection from young and unknown artists who sold their paintings for room and board. Some of them, such as Miró, Chagall, and Picasso, went on to achieve immortality. Steve's dream and desire of owning his own La Colombe d'Or was realized when he purchased the 21-room Fondren mansion, one of a group of homes in the Montrose area qualifying for the National Register of Historic Places.

The mansion was built on the outskirts of then downtown Houston in 1923 by Walter Fondren, founder of Humble Oil which later became part of Exxon. Fondren died in 1939, but Mrs. Fondren, who was 100 in June of 1980, lived in the mansion until the 1950s. She then allowed the American Red Cross to use her home free of charge as an office building. In came acoustical tile, linoleum rugs, and fluorescent glare.

When Zimmerman bought the mansion in 1979, he was faced with a monumental renovation. He had some help when he offered it to the Zeta Tau Alpha sorority to use as their 1980 Designers' Showcase benefit. Zimmerman retained some of the ideas the designers used, such as the painted cream and green floor which reflects the arabesques in the ceiling of one of the dining rooms. He also kept the intricate parquet floor of maple, cherry, mahogany, and oak in the entry parlor. But, the conversion from office building to a guest house and restaurant still cost a fortune.

The elegant entry parlor of the "smallest full-service luxury hotel in the United States."

Whatever the price, La Colombe d'Or is now a masterpiece of interior design and decor. The walls are hung with original canvases done by Houston artists. (This time the paintings are paid for in cash, not room and board.) Victorian, oriental, and modern furnishings all blend together. The antiques are all museum quality and the oriental rugs are the real thing.

Each suite is uniquely furnished and has its own private dining room.

The suites are appropriately named Monet, Cézanne, Renoir, Degas, and Van Gogh. Each suite has its own private dining room for intimate parties, and each is furnished with a different blend of gorgeous furniture. The Renoir Suite is decorated in oriental trappings. The Van Gogh is starkly modern with dark green walls, raised platform bed, chrome chairs, and huge white paintings.

When you check in to La Colombe d'Or, a crystal decanter of brandy, fresh fruit, and flowers await you. Breakfast in your private dining room is coffee or tea, freshly squeezed juice, and flaky hot croissants. Also available is limousine service, secretarial service, valet service, and even the use of the owner's private swimming pool. You do not even have to dial "9" before you make an outgoing call.

The library is now furnished with small tables and chairs as part of the bar and makes an ideal spot for an after-dinner port or cognac. Its fireplace is identical to the one in the main dining room. The bar itself is just off the entry parlor next to the library.

The restaurant has three really lovely dining rooms. Fresh flowers on every table, snowy linen, and gleaming crystal and silverware complement the French cuisine. Just a few of the many choices are pâte Colombe d'Or, escargots Bordelaise, pheasant Forestier (with chestnuts and mushrooms), Sautéed squid in lobster sauce, bouil-

La Colombe d'Or

labaisse, and steak tartare. There is also a special dish of rabbit sautéed in prune sauce. The wine list is most inclusive with vintages with $15 or $150. All selections are à la carte and expensive.

Everything about La Colombe d'Or is the epitome of small-hotel luxury, and every detail is perfect. Walter Fondren may have made millions, but there is no doubt he would be quite impressed with his mansion today.

Lamar Hotel

Main at Lamar
Houston, Texas 77002
Phone: 713-658-8511
Accommodations: 266 rooms
Rates: $48–$72

The Lamar Hotel's historic significance comes not from its architecture, nor from its age. This unimpressive square brick hotel was built in 1928 by the financial wizard Jesse Jones for the Democratic Convention. When the hotel was finished, Jesse moved into the sixteenth floor and lived there until he died in 1956.

Houston was Jones' town. He could look out of his sixteenth floor window and literally be lord of all he surveyed. In 1908 he put up the Bankers Mortgage Company building (then the Texas Company) and the Rusk Building (then the Gulf Building). In 1910 came the Houston Chronicle, and in 1912 what he thought was his masterpiece—the 18-story Rice Hotel. As long as Jones was alive the Rice was *the* hotel in Houston. The Rice became famous all over the country for its galas, its celebrities, and as the birthplace of many of Texas' biggest financial schemes. Jones also owned the Texas State Hotel and the McKinney Hotel, and until McCarthy built the Shamrock in 1949, Jesse Jones controlled the hotel business in Houston. But the Lamar was where he lived, and the Lamar was where he met with his friends to play cards, drink, and make deals. They met

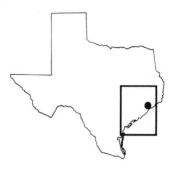

Diversions:

Astrodomain
Lyndon B. Johnson Space
*   Center*
Museum of Fine Arts
San Jacinto Battleground State
*   Historic Park*

in suite 8F, and before long they became known as the "8F Crowd," and the suite "the unofficial capitol of Texas."

It is interesting to speculate just how much Jones and his friends were worth. Jesse Jones owned most of what we call the "old downtown" of Houston, including the Texas Commerce Bank and more than 50 other properties in different parts of the United States. Judge James A. Elkins was the man behind the scenes controlling the city's largest law firm and First City National Bank. Both of his establishments often had the same clients—very powerful clients at that. George Brown, along with his brother Herman, owned the monstrous construction firm Brown & Root, and also one of the world's largest pipeline companies, Texas Eastern Transmission Company. If they ever had a question about insurance, all they had to do was ask Gus Wortham who owned American General, the state's largest insurance company.

The "8F Crowd" manipulated power, money, and men so cleverly that they not only controlled Houston, but their influence was felt throughout the rest of Texas as well. The direction Houston and Texas took was firmly set by these few men who called themselves "builders." It was these few strong men who made Texas and Houston their home, and they decided to make them great.

Lamar Hotel

Houston's original growth was spurred by the discovery of oil at Spindletop, but it was Jesse Jones who made her the great port she is today. When the government refused to finance the Ship Channel, Jones suggested that Houston put up half the money, and the government finance the rest. Hardly an innovative idea today, but back in those days it was most unusual. In 1914 President Wilson pressed the button from the White House that opened the Houston Ship Channel, and Houston, the major port, was born. Jones went on to become head of the powerful Reconstruction Finance Corporation under Franklin Roosevelt. After 13 years in Washington he returned to Houston, and the Lamar Hotel.

The Lamar no longer has a famous tenant, and the "8F Crowd" is now history. In spite of a $7-million face lift in 1969, the hotel is still an unimpressive edifice. As her manager, Eddie Davis, said, "The Lamar is where celebrities stay when they don't want anyone to know where they are."

The Lamar's days may well be numbered. She may not be Houston's most beautiful building, but in 1981 her real estate sold for Houston's record price of $400 – $500 a square foot. Purchased by Gerald Hines, it is quite plausible the hotel will go the way of most of "old downtown" and be replaced with modern offices and skyscrapers. Perhaps only Jones could save her now, but even if he were still around, it is doubtful he would make the effort. Never known for sentimentality, Jones would know a good deal when it arose. He and his "8F Crowd" would probably just move "the unofficial capitol of Texas" to another site worthy of their status.

Woodbine Hotel

209 N. Madison
Madisonville, Texas 77864
Phone: 713-348-3591
Accommodations: 9 rooms, all
with bath
Innkeepers:
Randy and Lynne Parton

The Woodbine—a beautiful name for a beautiful hotel. She was beautiful when she opened in 1904, and she is beautiful today. Built by a family of Russian Jews, it was originally the Shapira Hotel, and it remained in the Shapira family until 1929. When matriarch Sarah Shapira died, it was sold to Clara Wills. Mrs. Wills continued the high-quality family-style meals, but the hotel went into a decline. When the Partons acquired the building in 1979, the Shapira-Wills Hotel had fallen into almost total ruin.

It is difficult to believe the horror stories about the restoration that went into this building that is so gorgeous now. Weeds were so high that rooms on the ground floor were dark even at noon. Joe Pinnelli, who was in charge of restoration, said that "it reminded you of a Hitchcock story; it was scary to come in, even during the daylight." A great deal of the gingerbread trim on the outside was gone. Walls had been covered with asbestos siding, and the standing seam-tin roof had been covered with asphalt shingles. It took a great deal of imagination to see a beautiful lady under all that ugly covering.

The Woodbine is now well on her way to becoming one of the best of Texas inns. It is on the National Register of Historic Places for its significance as an example of Queen Anne Victorian architecture. The Woodbine has it all—turrets, gingerbread, "fishscale" shingles, and seven different colors of paint. Pinelli said, "This building looks like an angel food cake—with cherries on top!"

Inside are etched and stained glass windows done by Lynne Parton that look every bit like they were the ones installed in 1904. Floors have been stripped to their original pine, and all of the woodwork gleams with its true luster. The original fixtures had been stolen, so everything, even the doorknobs, had to be replaced. The only thing missing is the fireplace. Its chimney was so wobbly, it only took a slight push to knock it down. But the old bricks made a charming brick patio behind the lobby.

Woodbine Hotel

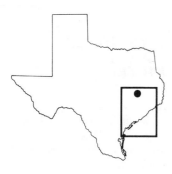

Built in the shape of a truncated "H", the hotel is flanked by two 3-story turrets. Downstairs, one of the turrets is a private club, The Rough Edge. It seems that back in 1901, Madisonville voted out demon rum and all the evils that went with it. However, the saloons and bars just moved right outside the city limits, and the edge of town soon became known as "The Rough Edge." Since Madisonville is still a dry town, the name of the Woodbine's private club couldn't be more *à propos*.

The downstairs of the other turret is part of the dining room. Not only is the hotel being restored, but the fabulous food is being restored as well. Research showed that Mrs. Shapira sat at a long table and presided over her dining room with as many as 30 hungry guests. Her daughters stood by and served fried chicken, country fried steak, ham, liver, blackeyed peas, fresh vegetables, biscuits, cornbread, homemade cakes, and cream pies. These same dishes, down to the homemade biscuits and cornbread, are served now to more hungry guests, and chicken is still fried in huge cast-iron skillets. The restaurant is open daily for lunch and dinner, and prices are reasonable.

Upstairs, the two turret rooms will be the prime guest quarters when completed (call for dates). All rooms will be done in Victorian wallpaper and period furniture, and all have a private bath.

Woodbine is an Old World name for the yellow honeysuckle. The word conjures up old-fashioned images of bygone days, and never have bygone days been so beautifully recaptured as at the Woodbine Hotel.

Luther Hotel

Palacios, Texas 77465
Phone: 512-972-2312
Accommodations 15 bedrooms
*   with bath; 24 apartments; 11*
*   motel rooms with kitchens; 1*
*   penthouse*
Rates: $20 + ; penthouse $50

Palacios was founded in 1903 in an area named by shipwrecked Spaniards who supposedly saw a vision of tres palacios (three palaces). Well, if the Luther Hotel had been there in the days of the Spaniards, it would have been one of the three palaces they saw. The elegant old Luther was built the year Palacios was founded, but not at its present site. Originally on East Bay, it was moved in 1905 one-half mile, and now it faces Tres Palacios Bay. Laboriously moved on skids, its chimneys were removed, porches torn down, and the entire structure hauled away in three sections. Today its circular drive is lined with palm trees, and a wide lawn stretches down to the bay. Built of solid cypress, this stately three-story hotel commands a really superb view.

The snowbirds from Yankeeland have long known how to find the Luther, and there is a "Return to Paradise" atmosphere among its extremely loyal clientele. It's very easy to see why, too, because this rambling old building and her owners, Mr. and Mrs. Luther, have a way of making guests feel truly welcome. No wonder so many northerners come here every winter, for the Luthers' hospitality is reminiscent of the antebellum South.

Most of the hotel has been converted to apartments which rent by the week or month, but the 15 overnight rooms all have ceiling fans, priscilla curtains, small baths, and antique furniture. Some rooms are air-conditioned, and all have a space heater, for it really does get a bit chilly even in Palacios. No TV or telephones are available in the rooms, so it's best to come with a good book or a very good friend. As Mrs. Luther says, "There will never be a TV in my guest rooms. I don't want people to come here to watch television."

Luther Hotel

Diversions:

Matagorda Beach
Aransas National Wildlife
Refuge
Hotel Blessing, Blessing, Texas

The only TV provided is downstairs in the charming little lobby which is more like a living room. Here some guests do gather in the evening to visit and watch TV for a while; however, most guests are found in the game room playing cards, visiting, and sharing home-made treats. It doesn't take long before you feel right at home and a part of the "Luther Hotel Family." Many of the "family" have been coming to the Luther for years and years, and Mrs. Luther said she often gets calls from members of her "family" that couldn't make it to Palacios that year to see how the rest of their group is faring.

One of the best features of the hotel (other than the Luthers) is the "penthouse." The third floor apartment is one of the best bargains in Texas. Done in fairly contemporary furniture, it has a sitting room, kitchen, large bedroom with a king-size bed, bath with a giant tub, and the only other color TV in the hotel. Best of all, it has the magnificent view of Tres Palacios Bay. The hotel roof is the penthouse porch, and it makes a most romantic spot to watch a sunset over the Bay. Mrs. Luther will rent to one couple only. No friends, no children are allowed, so you can lock the door and make the Luther penthouse your very special world with a very special person.

There is no hotel restaurant, but there are several cafes around Palacios that offer pretty good fare. Just don't expect any memorable meals.

A sign over the hotel's front desk reads, "He who enters here is a stranger but once," and after you've met the Luther's and their "family" you'll realize just how true this axiom is at the Luther Hotel.

Tarpon Inn

Box 8, Port Aransas, Texas
78373
Phone: 512-749-5555
Accommodations: 26 rooms, all
with bath
Rates: $30
Innkeeper: Jim Atwill

In spite of fire, hurricanes, and tropical storms, the indomitable old Tarpon Inn is still taking in guests. Located in a very vulnerable spot for hurricanes, she has survived in one form or another since 1886. Frank Stevenson originally built her of material from a Civil War barracks and named her for the abundant trophy fish in the surrounding waters. For years, Port Aransas was even known as "Tarpon."

The first disaster struck in 1900 when the hotel burned, but she was rebuilt in 1904. Then in 1919 a hurricane ripped away the main

Tarpon Inn

structure. When J. M. Ellis built her back in 1923, she resembled the old barracks of Civil War days. He put 20-foot poles in 16 feet of concrete, with piling at the corner of each room for reinforcement. No hurricane or storm has disturbed her since, and she has often served as a storm shelter without damage. The Tarpon Inn has more than earned her place on the National Register of Historic Places.

Many fishermen love to come to Port Aransas and try their luck catching the big game fish. Back in the old days they had to arrive at the Tarpon Inn by boat, since there wasn't any fast little Texas State Ferry to speed you across the Aransas Pass. In 1937 one very famous fisherman—Franklin D. Roosevelt—joined the ranks of others who traditionally signed and dated their tarpon scale to place on the wall in the lobby. There is even a wonderful 1937 photograph entitled, "President Roosevelt tells a fish story." His signed and dated scale has a place of honor among the hoards of others nailed to the wall, and the rooms he stayed in are now referred to as "The Presidential Suite."

Not much has changed since the 1920s except that the Tarpon's new coat of paint is blue-gray rather than the original white, and a cupola on the roof is no longer there. The best description of the Tarpon Inn's furnishings is "seaside tacky." All rooms have air-conditioning units and circular fluorescent lights dating back to some unknown year, and the rooms could easily handle a complete refurbishing. A wide veranda runs the entire length of the Inn both upstairs and down, and since there are no television sets or telephones, the best pastime is to sit on the veranda and watch tankers, yachts, and fishing boats sail in and out of the harbor.

If all that boat watching makes you hungry, the Tarpon Inn Restaurant is right behind the Inn in one of the 1919 buildings. Duncan Hines spent his honeymoon at the Tarpon Inn and for 25 years recommended the food here. If Duncan were alive today, he would still recommend it, for the food is excellent. Nothing is better than fresh seafood well prepared, and you can rest assured you'll have it all at the Tarpon Inn. Particularly good are the stuffed shrimp and the bowl of U-Peel-Um, all boiled, cold, and delicious. If you aren't sure just what a tarpon looks like, there is a stuffed one over the bar. The other restaurant walls display a gigantic marlin, a dolphin, a kingfish, an amber jack, a redfish, a sailfish, and a wahoo. The place is positively swimming in fish. Prices are moderate, and wine and bar drinks are available.

Jim Atwill, the Tarpon's innkeeper, has his personal theory of why people want to own a hotel. "I believe a hotel is an extension of your own hospitality. When you invite guests into your own place, you want to make them happy in a place you are happy in." There is no doubt you will be quite happy after a visit to the Tarpon Inn and its restaurant, for both have their own unique charm and should not be missed.

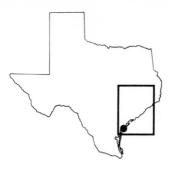

Diversions:

Aransas National Wildlife
   Refuge
Padre Island National Seashore
Corpus Christi

Central Texas

43

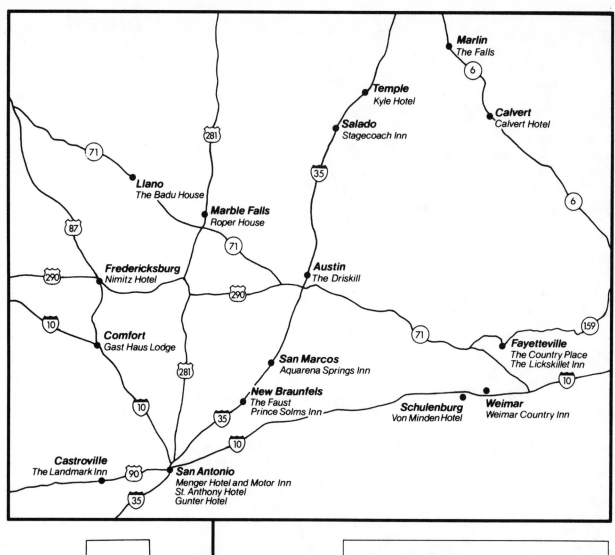

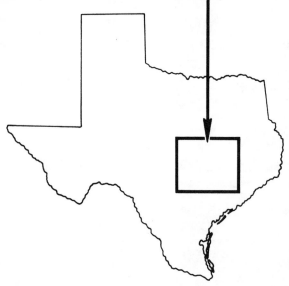

The Driskill

117 East 7th Street
Austin, Texas 78701
Phone: 1-800-252-9367
Accommodations: 180 rooms, all
*   with bath*
Rates $52-$92

The Driskill Hotel is probably more of a Texas institution than the State Capitol building, for The Driskill opened in December of 1886, and the Capitol wasn't completed until 1888. Certainly a great many political decisions have been made within The Driskill's walls, for since the day it opened it has been the gathering place of politicians, businessmen, and heads-of-state.

The Driskill began with the famous cattle baron, Colonel J. L. Driskill, who supplied beef to the Confederate forces during the Civil War. He built the finest hotel in the Southwest, and it became the outstanding attraction in Texas. Not only did this hotel offer gas lights and steam heat, but a special feature was the warm mineral water available to guests who believed it contained medicinal properties. This artesian well still supplies Austin's water.

So many "firsts" happened at The Driskill. It had the first electricity south and west of St. Louis. It had the first up-to-date call system. A guest could press a button in his room, a bell would ring in the office, and a bellman would hurry to the guest's room to be of service. The Driskill's elegant ballrom held the first inaugural ball in 1887 for Governor Sul Ross. The first telegraph office in Austin was at the hotel, and Austin's first long-distance telephone call was made from The Driskill to Wichita, Kansas. In 1909 the hotel even had its own fire department—the first fire department in Austin.

These days the Romanesque architecture of The Driskill is quite an anachronism in downtown Austin, with its rectangular steel, glass, and brick buildings. The hotel really is "old world grandeur in the heart of downtown Austin." With the resurgence of restoration on Sixth Street, a very popular area has been created with shops, bars, and restaurants. Most establishments reflect an atmosphere of nostalgia for Austin at the turn of the century. But The Driskill believes that Sixth Street begins at The Driskill. To emphasize this point, the new owners, Laral Hotels, Inc., have made a

Driskill Hotel

major change in the Cabaret. The discotheque with its garish modern decor and name no longer exist. Instead, The Driskill Bar now offers sedate, refined surroundings that reflect the tone the hotel wants to project. The Driskill Bar and Grill is actually the cornerstone of Sixth Street and intends to become the focal point of this section of old Austin.

Along with this new image, one-third of the rooms have been redecorated in period reproduction pieces, and wall coverings and carpets have been replaced. Throughout her many owners, The Driskill's rooms have been totally lacking in charm until this recent change. Laral Hotels, Inc. plans to continue this scheme until all the rooms are finished. The LBJ Suite still offers furnishings of the very finest, and The Bungalow on the roof can be rented for a mere $475 per night. Colonel Driskill's great-grandson and great-great-grandson were on hand to dedicate The Bungalow, which is now referred to as the "Best Little Penthouse in Texas."

The Driskill lobby has been privy to the conversations of politicians, businessmen, and heads-of-state.

The Driskill Dining Room is one of Austin's most famous and favorite restaurants.

The famous Victorian piano bar in the lobby is unchanged with its ornate, carved wood panel ceiling, floral carpeting, and fine oils. It is still the place in Austin where people go who want to be seen.

Tiffany chandeliers, brocade upholstry, and shining brass still enhance the elegant atmosphere of The Driskill Dining Room. Old World cuisine as well as Texas-style meals make it one of Austin's most famous restaurants. There is just no telling what famous person or well-known politician you are likely to see dining at one of the tables.

An outstanding group event can be scheduled in the magnificent Maximilian Room where the eight gold-leaf mirrors that once belonged to Mexico's Imperial Majesties Carlotta and Maximilian are displayed. These mirrors were the wedding gift of Maximilian to Carlotta (reported to be the most beautiful woman in Europe). Atop each mirror is a gilt medallion likeness of the Empress. Beaded crystal chandeliers and imported dark red tapestries offset the beauty of these famous mirrors.

Austin has come a long way from the cowtown with unpaved streets, and she is now the town that Colonel Driskill envisioned so many years ago. His wonderful hotel has survived magnificently in spite of all the changes to his city and to his building. The Driskill has become a tradition with Texas leaders, Congressmen, businessmen, and families. The Driskill Hotel *is* Texas.

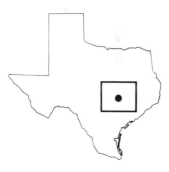

Diversions:

Governor's Mansion
Laguna Gloria Art Museum
Lyndon B. Johnson Library and
  Museum
State Capitol complex
The University of Texas at
  Austin

Calvert Hotel

P. O. Box 785
Calvert, Texas 77837
Phone: 713-364-2501
Accommodations: 5 rooms, 1
  bath; 2 suites with bath
Rates: $20–$25
Innkeepers: Glenn and Edith
  Murphy

The Calvert Hotel looks like it should be a plantation mansion in the Deep South rather than an inn in a sleepy little Central Texas town. It does not miss being antebellum by many years. Built in 1872, this lovely old southern-style mansion with its Doric columns is once again open for guests.

A succession of owners tried various projects with the Calvert Hotel, and for a while it was even a dinner theatre. Now the new owners are turning it back into an inn. The Murphys became innkeepers quite by accident. They were in the market for an old Victorian house, and everything they found was out of their budget. They were offered the Calvert Hotel at a price less than a house, because it had been standing vacant for several years. Unable to resist such a prize, the Murphys and their guests will all benefit from their unexpected bargain.

The Murphys have turned the entry hall and parlor into a homey living room. It is filled with overstuffed furniture and lots of charming knick-knacks; the overall effect is very comfortable clutter. There is a game table, a television set, and lots of good conversation with the hosts.

The hotel has no restaurant, but Edith has added some real personal touches to your stay. For about $2.50 she fixes a sumptuous breakfast with ham, eggs, homemade preserves, and homemade biscuits with gravy. The coffee is always freshly brewed by 5:30 a.m., and all of this is served at a big antique dining room table with real Texas hospitality.

On your way out to dinner, listen to Edith's advice when she cautions you not to have dessert, because she prepares a special treat for you to be served with coffee in the living room when you return.

Calvert Hotel

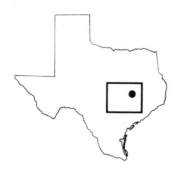

There is no charge; it is just the Murphys delightful way of saying they are glad you are staying with them.

Guest rooms are furnished with iron double beds, old dressers, and bright new bedspreads. Curtains are springy and fresh, and Victorian style light fixtures add to the decor. All are centrally heated and air-conditioned. A bath for ladies and one for men are down the hall.

Some of the rooms are named. The Whitfield Cain room is named for a prominent doctor who was the hotel's first registered guest. The Robert Calvert room is named for the founder of the town who was a descendant of Lord Baltimore. The Robert E. Lee room needs no explanation, and the last name on a door is Gottlich Dirr, the builder of the hotel.

Why one of the suites is called the Governor's Suite is unknown, so the Murphys hung a picture of Edmund Davis on the wall, as he was governor of Texas when the hotel was built in 1872. They also wrote to Governor Clements and told him about the suite, and his picture and his reply are on the wall, too. This suite has a small kitchen, its own bath, a double bed, and also a single bed.

Calvert prides itself on being "The Antique Capital of Texas," and not only does it have antique shops, it also has numerous old buildings, homes, and churches, some of which were built before the Civil War. During Reconstruction days, Calvert was the site of an unusual prison—a "sky parlor" platform jail built atop a tall pole to hold Southern sympathizers. Today, Calvert hosts several pilgrimages a year through its historic buildings, and the Calvert Hotel is sure to become the star attraction on the tour.

Qu' tient à sa tranquilliré sait respecter celles des autres.
(He who values his own tranquility knows how to respect that of others.)

Motto in old inn at Alsace, France

The Landmark Inn

U. S. 90, Castroville, Texas
P. O. Box 577, Castroville,
Texas 78009
Phone: 512-538-2133
Accommodations: 8 rooms, 6
baths

A replica of this old Alsatian sampler hangs in every room of The Landmark Inn. The motto could not be more appropriate, for tranquility is certainly valued in this old inn. Even though The Landmark is right off busy Highway 90, its old buildings with their thick walls act as a buffer against outside noise. Beautiful grounds with flowers, trees, and a splashing fountain create an idyllic Alsatian setting, and you are immediately transported to a part of old France.

No place in Texas is quite as unique as Castroville. The town's rare qualities are a result of its founder, Henri Castro. Castro was a French Jew of Spanish/Portuguese ancestry, and was an entrepreneur of the same type as Stephen F. Austin. Whereas Austin secured land grants from Mexico, Castro dealt with The Republic of Texas. Texas was anxious to prevent Mexican infiltrations of her territory, so in 1842 Castro was awarded a section of land just west of San Antonio. His standards for colonists were so high he had difficulty in recruiting the new settlers. Few immigrants had the necessary $32 passage money, plus reserve funds for unforeseen disasters, and their own tools. After many setbacks, Castro finally arrived in Texas with his little group, and in September of 1844, Castroville became a reality.

Most of the colonists came from Alsace, a French province on the German border that was a source of constant dispute between the two countries. The new settlers brought with them their unrecorded language, their architecture, and their love of feasting to the wilderness of Texas to create a rare heritage. Their tiny cottages of river rock and cypress beams look like they should be nestled on the banks of the Rhine River rather than the Medina.

In 1880 the Southern Pacific Railroad bypassed Castroville, and the little community became locked in time. Perhaps it was for the best, for progress has a way of destroying what is old and getting on with the new, and Castroville's uniqueness may have been lost forever. Now there are almost 100 perfectly preserved architectural examples of life in early Castroville.

The Landmark Inn, constructed about 1849, is as steeped in history as the town itself. As most inns of this type, it began as a stage stop on the way to San Antonio. Several buildings make up the complex, one of which was the old bathhouse. Its lead lining was removed during the Civil War to make bullets for the Confederacy. Now this two-story bathhouse has a small guest room on both floors, each with a single bed and private bath.

The main building has one guest room downstairs and five on the second floor. All rooms are charmingly decorated with dressers, iron beds, wardrobes, and funky lamps. The furnishings are more 20th Century than 19th. A few rooms have wall-to-wall carpeting, and all have ceiling fans and air-conditioning. There are no TV sets nor telephones to mar the inn's tranquility.

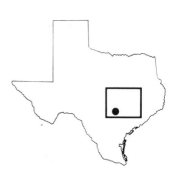

Diversions:

Historic area of Castroville
San Antonio
Scenic Texas Hill Country

Landmark Inn

The Landmark does not have a restaurant, but there is Sammy's close by on Highway 90 that features local specialties and good home cooking. Haby's Alsatian Bakery, also on U.S. 90, is known all over the state for its French breads and pastries.

Now the property of the State of Texas, The Landmark was a welcome donation to the Parks Service. Closed for many years, it is once again welcoming guests. No doubt Castroville will become a tourist attraction much as New Braunfels and Fredericksburg—however this time with a French flavor. Merci, Henri Castro, for bringing a part of your world to Texas.

Gast Haus Lodge

944 High Street
Comfort, Texas 78013
Phone: 512-995-2304

Local historians have constructed the following account of the naming of Comfort. When a group of free-thinking Germans arrived here at the confluence of Cypress Creek and the Guadalupe River, they agreed that this was a great *gemütlicher platzt* to settle. *Gemütlich* translates as "comfortable," and was later shortened to Comfort.

When the Civil War came to Texas, these stubborn German pioneers refused to join the Confederacy. On their way to Mexico in an attempt to join the Union Army, 36 were killed by Confederate forces in the 1862 Nueces River Massacre. Other than national cemeteries, Comfort has the only monument to the Union in Confederate territory. This *Treue der Union* or "loyal to the Union" monument was erected on the common grave of these men.

Tucked away in tiny Comfort is the Gast Haus Lodge. The first building in the complex was built about 1857 and served as a stagecoach stop. It is the building nearest the street. Next to it was built a "lying-in" maternity hospital for pregnant women on their way from their ranches to San Antonio. The rock building in the center

Gast Haus

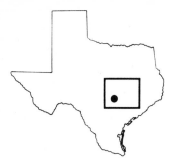

Diversions:

*Most complete 19th Century
    business district still standing
    in Texas*

was completed about 1869, and the white colonial-style house was built specifically to serve the new railroad in 1887. Known as the Meyer Hotel, it became the Gast Haus in 1973.

For romance it is hard to beat a Texas Hill Country moon, and the most romantic spot to spoon is in the gazebo in the Gast Haus garden. On the really lovely grounds are also a swimming pool and creek. Rooms are plain with old furniture, but extremely clean and charming. All have their own bath and air-conditioning. Some of the rooms have been converted into permanent apartments, so the number of guest rooms actually available may change.

About the only place to eat in Comfort is the Cypress Creek Inn. Although absolutely plain with chrome chairs and plastic tablecloths, its food is famous throughout the Hill Country. *Roadfood* rates Cypress Creek Inn with four stars for its country cooking at inexpensive prices.

A gazebo, a pool, good food, and a Hill Country moon—what more could you ask for a perfect escape!

The Country Place

*On the Square
Fayetteville, Texas 78940
Phone: Houston 713-522-0777;
    Fayetteville 713-378-2712
Accommodations: 6 rooms, 2
    baths
Rates: $15
Innkeepers: Clovis and
    Maryann Heimsath*

Nestled in the rolling hills of south central Texas, Fayetteville is a perfect getaway. Time just seems to stand still in this bucolic setting. The Country Place inn is appropriately named, for that is just what the entire town of Fayetteville is—a country place.

The Country Place is in the Zapp building, which was constructed in 1900. Located in the corner of the square, it was the Zapp General Store. Over the years boarders and drummers lived in the upstairs bedrooms. Then for a while it was a hospital, but the only reminder is a medical emblem painted on the south brick wall. Today, the offices of Clovis Heimsath Associates, Architects, occupy the mercantile part of the building. The upstairs is once again used for guest rooms, with one bath for ladies and one for gentlemen. The ladies bath has a tub the size of a horse trough.

A great deal of the charm of The Country Place is its informality. There is a list posted as to which room is yours and a register to

Country Place Hotel

sign, but then you are on your own. There are no keys, just hook-and-eye locks. Nor is there any air-conditioning—you are totally dependent on Mother Nature—but the windows are screened. The best room is No. 4; it is a large corner room with a good breeze.

Rooms are furnished in basic old pieces without any adornment, but they have a really terrific charm. The upstairs parlor opens onto the second floor veranda, which is a wonderful place to watch a sunrise, or just to sit and watch Fayetteville leisurely pass in review. There is absolutely nothing pretentious about The Country Place, yet it is one of the most popular weekend retreats in Texas.

The Country Place Restaurant prides itself on casual atmosphere and superb food. On the first floor of the Zapp Building, it is open on Friday and Saturday for dinner and for brunch on Sunday. It has a fixed menu for each meal, but the menu varies each day. A typical dinner is vichyssoise, a green salad, chicken crêpes with broccoli in cheese sauce, dessert and coffee, all for a moderate price. The restaurant is operated by Carol and Perry Thacker and offers yet another great reason to come to Fayetteville.

A stroll around the square is a must. All the buildings have a story, and the Red and White Store (which is now blue) may be the oldest building in Fayetteville. Schramm's Confectionary Bar is certainly more a bar than it is a confectionary. And just on the edge of town is one of the best cemeteries in Texas. Ornate tombstones with actual pictures of the deceased typify the Czech influence in this section of Texas. Fayetteville has even been called "the cradle of Czech heritage in Texas."

It is always difficult to leave the peace and serenity of this little town and return to reality, but at least you know that when you do return, nothing will have changed, and Fayetteville will be just the way you left it.

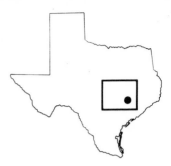

Diversions:

Henkel Square and Festival Hill, Round Top, Texas
Brazos Belle Inn, country cooking in Burton, Texas

The Lickskillet Inn

Just off the Square
P. O. Box 85, Fayetteville, Texas 78940
Phone: 713-378-2846
Accommodations: 3 rooms, 1 bath
Rates: $30-$35
Innkeepers: Steve and Jeanette Donaldson

With a population of just over 400, Fayetteville is one of the most perfect small towns in Texas. Incorporated in 1882, it hasn't changed a great deal since then. City folks love to come here and experience the aura of small-town living, and the ideal spot to do this is The Lickskillet Inn.

If you are wondering about the name, proprietress Jeanette Donaldson is quite a history buff and says the story goes like this. Back in the 1820s folks in this part of the country used to hold free feasts to draw them closer together to work on community projects. At one such feast the gathering ran out of food, and a witty cook remarked to the latecomers they would have to "lick the skillet clean." The phrase stuck and evolved into "lickskillet." The area was even called "Lickskillet" before P. J. Shaver christened the town Fayetteville in 1847. So the inn's name is even older than its structure.

The Lickskillet Inn

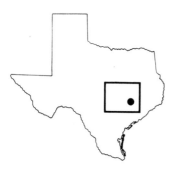

Diversions:

*Brazos Belle Inn, superb
   country food, Burton, Texas
Old Czech cemetery
Fayetteville town square
Henkel Square and Festival
   Hill, Round Top*

Built in 1853, this Evans-Steves house (named for the first owner and also the longest owner) has everything it takes to enjoy the full ambience of a small country town's atmosphere. The white picket fence, the hammock in the front yard, porch swings, and rocking chairs make The Lickskillet the ideal spot to savor the advantages of a small community.

The inn's three bedrooms are absolutely delightful. Each room has an antique double bed covered with old quilts. However, underneath is a practical electric blanket for comfort in the winter. Large wardrobes, dressers with crocheted doilies, and antique chairs and tables complete the furnishings. The Donaldsons have put personal touches everywhere, and old bric-a-brac and pictures add to the decor. Ceiling fans whir in the summer to make the air-conditioning more efficient, and pot-bellied stoves glow in the winter to knock the chill. When you arrive there is a note on your door advising that the room has been especially reserved just for you.

The hallway was originally the dog run. Now it is transformed into a treasure-trove of memorabilia, with even an ancient dictaphone. The community bath is at the end of the hall, with a footed tub, walls and ceilings of green tin plate, and a simple key latch. Towards the rear of the inn is the dining room and kitchen. A continental breakfast of coffee, tea, and homemade bread comes with the room, and the first person up plugs in the coffee pot.

Even the inn's sign is clever. Under Lickskillet Inn either of these messages are added: "There is room at the inn," or "There is no room at the inn." With luck, you are rocking on the front porch when the "no room at the inn" sign goes up.

Fredericksburg is one of the most picturesque towns in Texas. Established in 1846, its German founders named it for Prince Frederick of Prussia. Not only does it have a large number of recorded Texas landmarks, but a major portion of the downtown area is listed in the National Register of Historic Places. One of the town's most unusual buildings on Main Street is the Nimitz Steamboat Hotel.

Charles Nimitz had been a sailor on German merchant ships, and he came to Fredericksburg with the original German settlers. He and his wife, Sophie, opened their hotel in 1852 with only four rooms. A few years later they added the famous Steamboat addition which made the hotel look like a giant ship chugging down Main Street. The Steamboat was "modernized" into a conventional hotel in the 1920s, and the crow's nest removed. Today the Nimitz has been completely restored, and once again the famous Steamboat addition dominates downtown Fredericksburg.

The Nimitz served as a spa for isolated ranchers, traders, and bored army personnel. The hotel had the frontier's first bathhouse, and with its tin tubs it must have been as popular as the saloon. Mother Nimitz's true talent was in the kitchen, though; and her table was known from Texas to California. Naturally, the famous hotel attracted important guests. Generals Longstreet and Robert E. Lee stayed here before the Civil War, and General Phil Sheridan after the war. It even hosted President Rutherford B. Hayes while enroute to Mexico.

Charles Nimitz was destined to have a descendant equally as famous as his hotel guests. His grandson was born in 1885, and Chester inherited his grandfather's love of the sea. He reached the highest rank in the United States Navy and commanded the Pacific Fleet in World War II. Japanese historians regard Nimitz as one of the three greatest admirals of all time, with only Lord Nelson and Japan's Togo in his class.

Today the Nimitz Steamboat Hotel is part of the Admiral Nimitz Center, which is actually three museums. Not only is it a memorial

Nimitz Steamboat Hotel

*340 East Main
Fredericksburg, Texas 78624
Accommodations: Museum only
Hours: Daily 8:00 a.m. to 5:00
p.m.
Admission: $1.00*

Nimitz Hotel

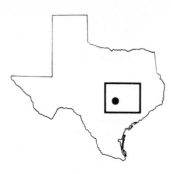

Diversions:

Balanced Rock
Pioneer Museum
Historic Fredericksburg
Lyndon B. Johnson State and
*   National Parks*

to one of Texas' most famous sons, but it is also a memorial of World War II and a history of Fredericksburg as well. The museum highlights Admiral Nimitz's career from the U. S. Naval Academy through Pearl Harbor to winning the war.

One of the best features of the World War II memorabilia is that you are allowed to touch many of the displays. A whole ship's steerage is set up, and you can actually experience steering a vessel. You can sit in all the gunners' positions on the gun emplacements. There is even an operational command center where you can see a battle unfolding. Another interesting exhibit is a replica of the atom bomb that ended the war.

The Nimitz Museum has a number of relics of the Pacific campaigns on view in an open area two blocks from the museum proper. There is a light tank the Japanese used when fighting on the Pacific islands, and the wreckage of a Japanese dive bomber, the type used during the attack on Pearl Harbor.

Next to the Center is one of the loveliest gardens in Texas. This small plot was a gift of the Japanese government to honor Admiral Nimitz, and special Japanese gardeners were sent to Fredericksburg to create it for the museum. It is appropriately named the Peace Garden.

Even though the Nimitz is no longer a hotel, it has become one of the finest museums in Texas. With a little imagination you can see Granpa Charles standing on the crow's nest of his Steamboat Hotel, pleased as he can be with the rich history he brought to his new home in Texas.

The Badu House

Highway 71 North
Llano, Texas 78643
Accommodations: 8 rooms, 7
*   baths (write for opening date)*
Rates: $30-$45
Innkeepers: Ann and Earl Ruff

On December 8, 1891, Francis Fisher signed a contract with the First National Bank of Llano to erect a granite and brick building within 45 days for the sum of $5,300.00. It is unknown whether Francis Fisher met his deadline or had to pay $10 for every day after that until it was completed; but he did his work well, regardless of the length of time. This classic old building of Italian Renaissance Palace character has weathered her years beautifully. Its great simplicity and blocky outline represent an exceptional example of the use of native design talent and materials of construction. The almost ornate Victorian-type, checkerboard texture band above the windows on both floors is a unique use of local granite. Because of the adaptation of classical forms in floor plan and facade and the use of these strong native materials, The Badu House was awarded a place on the National Register of Historic Places.

After the bank failed, the building was purchased by Professor N. J. Badu in 1898. Badu was a French mineralogist who discovered the rare opaline stone found only in Llano county. He and his family turned the bank into their private residence and his descendants lived there until it was sold to the Ruffs in 1980.

Many of the original bank features are still intact. The marble floor in the front room was part of Francis Fisher's contract, and the hinges, door handles, and window pulls are all made of solid brass with a distinctive flower motif. This flower motif is carried throughout The Badu House. The upstairs was eight bank offices divided by handsome oak partitions. The partitions are still there and will be used in the remodeling of the guest rooms.

The new role of The Badu House is that of country inn, restaurant, and private club. Downstairs are three dining rooms, all elegantly wallpapered, with the original lighting fixtures still in use. Shades of gray, pink, and white are the main colors of the dining rooms. Lace curtains do not hide the unusual shutters on the windows that were installed when the bank was built. Rather than opening out, the shutters are in three panels that slide up and down. China is used in all place settings, and the flatware is mixed patterns of old silverplate. Lace tablecloths, old china pieces, and candlelight complete the tone of subdued elegance. Antique sideboards are serving stations, and potted plants, ceiling fans, and wicker flower baskets with fresh flowers add to the Victorian atmosphere of the rooms.

Ann is the chef of The Badu House and prepares a different menu each day. There may be smothered steak, braised beef tips, roast beef, chicken and dumplings or some other good country dish. Her specialty is corn bread fried in thin cakes almost like crêpes—yet crisp and delicious. Open everyday from 11 a.m. to 10 p.m., lunch consists of homemade soups, salads, and sandwiches, and there is also a luncheon special. There is a fixed menu for dinner, with an appetizer, salad, entrée, vegetables, and desert, or your choice of a steak or selected seafoods.

Entry to the restaurant and club is on the side of the building under a canopy with the simple statement "The Badu House." As you enter, immediately facing you is a gorgeous stairway leading to the guest rooms. On your left is a small parlor done in Victorian decor and also a beautiful pump organ more than 100 years old that guests are welcome to play. Next to the parlor is the Legal Tender Saloon with an antique stained glass and mirrored back bar. It offers intimate seating and good drinks. Earl is the bartender when he is in Llano. Temporary memberships are available for a nominal fee.

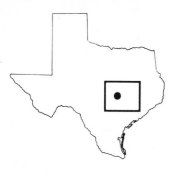

Diversions:

*Enchanted Rock State Park
Lakes Buchanan, Inks, and
    L.B.J.
The Llano Uplift, a rockhound's
    heaven*

From the bar, you can go out onto a wooden deck area and have cocktails and dinner in the garden. The garden's old-fashioned landscaping and fountain make this a delightful spot to enjoy the Texas Hill Country's invigorating air. Still standing in the garden is the playhouse Professor Badu built for his children, and Ann has put her own childhood keepsakes and other old toys on its shelves.

In the rear of The Badu House are the ruins of an old wall and store that was part of Llano in the late 1800s. Earl has left the entire structure intact and built a room within these stone walls to be his office. One entire wall of the office is lined with shelves crammed with souvenirs from all parts of the world. The other walls display spears and shields from Kenya, masks from Indonesia, swords from Spain, and bolos from Argentina. The Ruffs are great travelers and also collectors of odd and unusual art objects from different countries.

The upstairs will soon be remodeled into eight guest rooms and seven baths. All will be furnished with iron beds, marble-top washstands, wardrobes, and lace curtains. One wall will be a panel from the old bank offices, and the other walls will be wallpapered. Pressed tin ceilings and paddle fans are to be added, and the rooms will be named rather than numbered. The Aberdeen Room, named for Ann's hometown in Mississippi, is to be done in Westlake Victorian pieces that were left to her by her great-grandmother. The walls will be hung with Ann's family portraits and photographs of Aberdeen personalities taken many years ago. Other bric-a-brac from Mississippi will add little personal touches to each room. Crocheted doilies on the chairs and hand-embroideried dresser scarves and pillow cases were done by Ann's mother for the inn. Baths are small, but each comes with its own claw-foot bathtub, pedestal wash basin, and pull-chain toilet.

Restoration of any old bulding is always filled with headaches, hidden expenses, disappointments, and unexpected diasters. The Badu House had her share of all of these, but she has emerged magnificent and elegant. Francis Fisher truly earned his $5,300.00, because he built The Badu House to last forever.

Roper House

*Highway 281 at 3rd
P. O. Box 788
Marble Falls, Texas 78654
Phone: 512-693-5561
Accommodations: Restaurant
    only
Hosts: Ronald and Merianne
    Wininger*

The Hotel de Roper is a building quite neat,
And the fare they give you is hard to beat.
The Drummers say Uncle George is clever and kind.
And Mrs. Roper as hostess is just to one's mind.

Marble Falls Messenger, December 1899

If this unknown author were writing today, all he would have to do is change the name of the hosts, for Roper House is still "quite neat" and the fare "hard to beat." George and Elizabeth Hockenhull

Roper have been replaced by Ronald and Merianne Wininger, but the rest of the ditty is just as accurate as it was in 1899.

The Roper Hotel was built by George and Elizabeth about 1880. They migrated to Texas in the late 1870s via Missouri, Kansas, and Georgia. When they arrived in Marble Falls, they settled down to stay. Marble Falls was being promoted as "The Manufacturing Center of the Southwest" in those years, and nearby quarries furnished the granite for the new State Capitol, the Galveston Seawall, and the fishing jetties along the Gulf Coast.

This sturdy, no-nonsense building was made of locally manufactured brick, with rusticated granite sills and architraves from a local quarry. One rather unusual detail for a Texas building in this era consisted of *voussoirs*, window sills and trim at the sides and rear of the building, covered in stained mastic to simulate brownstone. The owner's quarters, kitchen, and dining room were on the first floor, with 12 guest rooms upstairs. A picket fence enclosed the yard to keep out the meandering cattle.

As one of the earliest hotels in this part of Texas, the Roper served as a weekend stopover for Texas governors and politicians. It was also a stage stop and headquarters for drummers. Governor Hogg and his entourage are said to have taken excursions to Marble Falls on the railroad, held festivities on the steamer (owned by Roper's brother, W. H.), frequented the saloons, and stayed at the Roper Hotel.

The Ropers sold the hotel in 1926, and it became the Central Hotel. In 1937 it became the Francis House and went through a refurbishing which included adding modern bathrooms. Finally, in 1963 it was purchased by Don and Michelle Gunn. Don's family had been a part of Marble Falls for generations. When there was talk of making the Roper into a savings and loan, he and Michelle felt there would be nothing left of the town's past for their children to see. Michelle had grown up only a few blocks from the hotel and had played there as a child. Neither she nor Don could bear to see it destroyed.

Thanks to the Gunns, the Roper has a long and bright future ahead. Placed on the National Register of Historic Places, the Roper Hotel is now the Roper House. The Gunns have gone to great ex-

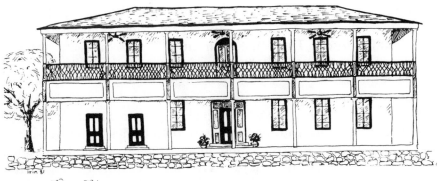

Roper House

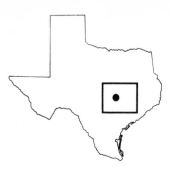

Diversions:

Granite Mountain
Scenic Drive R.M. 1431
Lake Marble Falls

tremes to see that the exterior is as close to the original as possible, but the interior is a whole new world. The Gunns have leased the building to the Winingers who own and operate Roper House as a restaurant and private club.

The club has maroon fabric wall coverings and maroon carpet highlighted by light blue upholstered chairs and crystal chandeliers. The downstairs dining room has the natural brick walls, an 1800s floral pattern wallpaper, and pale pink tablecloths and napkins. There are shades on the windows, brass chandeliers, ceiling fans, and potted plants. Restaurant chairs were hand-picked in sets from a Houston antique dealer, and antique sideboards are serving stations. A working fireplace on the rear wall will add to the charm of the room in cold weather.

The stairwell is hung with old pictures of Marble Falls and of the Roper. At the head of the stairway is a wonderful photograph of George and Elizabeth Roper beaming their approval of what has been accomplished with their hotel.

The upstairs is composed of two large dining rooms, and the decor is much the same as it is downstairs, with the entire interior expertly coordinated in color scheme and furnishings. Also upstairs is a balcony with hanging baskets, ceiling fans, and rocking chairs for before and after-dinner drinks. Another delightful spot is the patio garden for dining under a Hill Country moon. Its herbs supply the spices for the kitchen.

Roper House not only has atmosphere, it also has a master chef, John Von Kaenel, who prepares a French menu. Poulet aux champignons, Veau Bretton, and Medallions de Veau Francais are all standard fare, and Boeuf Wellington and Le Chateaubriand will be prepared with 24-hour notice.

A modern poet would no doubt wax much more poetic than "quite neat" and "hard to beat" about the Roper House, but those plain 1899 words quaintly sum up the restaurant as nicely now as they did when they were written.

The Faust

240 S. Seguine
New Braunfels, Texas 78130
Phone: 512-625-7791
Accommodations: 62 rooms, all
*   with bath*
Price Range: $28-$43

The 1920s were big years for hotel construction in Texas, and quite a few hotels bear striking similarities. Architecturally the hotels are functional boxes built out of tacky yellow or garish red bricks, but each has its distinctive features, and all represent a marvelous era that is gone forever. The Faust, built in 1928, has the tacky yellow brick; and to re-visit the 1920s, all you have to do is stay in this wonderful hotel.

When The Faust was built it was named The Traveler's Inn, but during World War II it became the Honeymoon Hotel. Men stationed at nearby San Antonio came with their brides for a three-day-pass honeymoon. Later, the Honeymoon Hotel went bankrupt and the local bank gained ownership. The hotel was then named The

Faust after the president of the bank at that time. The last owner before its renovation was Bob Krueger, ambassador to Mexico under President Carter. Now the property of a Houston firm, The Faust was restored in 1978.

Today The Faust is one of the best examples of a restored hotel in the state. There were the usual major problems of re-wiring the entire building, overhauling the plumbing and heating, and adding air-conditioning. Also, all the ancient radiators and pipes had to be removed, custom-built fire doors added and 306 windows replaced. A new elevator was installed, but the 1928 cab was retained. As a result of all the careful renovation work, The Faust is once again a handsome hotel.

The minute you step into the lobby, you realize The Faust is a special hotel. The decor is almost an exact duplicate of what it was in the 1920s. Back in that era the use of decorative tile was very popular, and The Faust has one of the most ornate and intrically designed tile floors still in existence. The tiles continue up the stairway to the second floor. Victorian and 1920s furniture, which includes some of the hotel's original pieces, adds to the charm of the lobby. The old ceiling fans still whirr, and the big cash register has been ringing up sales since The Faust opened.

Each guest room is provided an individual touch with armoires, dressers, and odd bits and pieces found in the hotel when renovation began. Paddle fans in all of the rooms were installed when The Faust was built, and they still create the 1920s atmosphere, but air-conditioning has been added, along with TV sets. Another feature not found in many old hotels is a candlestick telephone in each room.

Some of the rooms are quite small and the baths downright teensy-tiny, but this is characteristic of most hotels during this period. The bathrooms have floors of the little six-sided tiles you only see in bathrooms built in the twenties and thirties, and the old por-

Faust Hotel

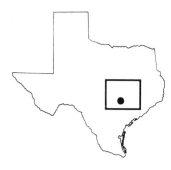

celain fixtures are still there, too. Some even have claw-footed tubs. The one suite has a sitting room with a bar and comfortable chairs around an antique table, a bedroom, and a bath. Another room can be opened on to this if needed.

Just off the lobby is the Veranda Restaurant, which re-creates the era of The Faust with its latticework, green plants, hanging baskets, and bentwood chairs. It offers all-day dining at moderate prices. There is a country-style breakfast with great homemade biscuits, and lunch and dinner feature steaks, burgers, and German sausage. The menu is cleverly presented on a fan—after all, every veranda needs a fan.

When The Faust re-opened in 1978 there was an attractive patio behind the hotel. It has since been glassed in and made into a nice-size bar. Subdued and intimate with good drinks, it is a favorite place for New Braunfels' residents as well as hotel guests.

The Faust, with all its ambience and charm, is once again a wonderful hotel for a honeymoon, and its lobby has provided a perfect setting for several weddings. But *every* visit to The Faust is a treasured memory, no matter what the occasion. You fervently wish there were many more of these old hotels being restored and offering hospitality of a bygone era, but at least there is The Faust for a trip back in time.

Prince Solms Inn

295 East San Antonio
New Braunfels, Texas 78130
Phone: 512-625-9169
Accommodations: 8 rooms, all
with bath; 2 suites
Rates $42-$85
Innkeepers: Marge Crumbaker
and Betty Mitchell

The Prince Solms is a jewel of an inn in a jewel of a town. The old German pioneers who settled here named their town for the place of their origin, Braunfels on the Lahn River, Germany. Led by the aristocratic Prince Carl of Solms-Braunfels, the immigrants arrived at the junction of the Comal and Guadalupe Rivers in 1845. With typical German skill and determination, the settlement prospered. However, within a few months, Prince Carl, who was somewhat of a dandy, became disillusioned and returned to Germany and his

Prince Solms Inn

fiancée, Princess Sophie. New Braunfels, with its rich German heritage, became a major asset to the new state of Texas.

When the hotel was built in 1898 and 1899, it was known as the Comal Hotel, named for the only river in the U. S. that begins and ends in the same city. All materials came from the area. The soft-colored beige bricks were made only a few miles away on the Guadalupe River and hauled to the site in wagons. The lumber was cut from giant cypress trees which line the banks of the Guadalupe, and all of the craftsmen were of German descent.

The builder was a man whose family had immigrated with Prince Carl, and his name was Christian Herry. Herry decided to build an inn which would last. The footings are 36 inches wide, narrowing to 18 inches above ground. Architectural students come from all over the country on field trips to study the construction and admire

The exquisite hall and staircase show the pride with which Prince Solms Inn was restored.

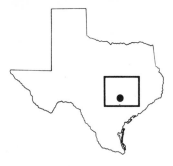

Diversions:

Guadalupe and Comal Rivers
Landa Park
Sophienburg Museum
Canyon Lake
Gruene Hall, Gruene, Texas

the beauty of the well-proportioned building in relationship to its height, windows, and doors.

The Comal later became the Prince Solms, and it has been an operating hotel almost continuously since it was built. Sturdy and plain on the outside, the interior is exquisite. The first-floor ceilings are 14 feet high, and those on the second floor are 11 feet. A skylight assures that the hotel is always bright and cheery. All of the hardware on the doors and hinges is made of orange bronze rather than brass as most old fittings. The furnishings are an antique lover's dream, for her owners are so proud of the hotel they have decorated every room and the parlor with expensive and beautiful pieces.

The names of the guest rooms tickle the imagination; most were named for their wallpaper pattern. The Rose, Magnolia, Huntsman, Songbird, Peony, and Summerhouse have double beds; the Penelope contains twin beds; and the Library is the only room with a king-size bed. The Library, appropriately, has a wall lined with bookshelves. The two suites are on the first floor and named the Prince Carl and the Sophie Suites. Not only are the suites luxurious, but the breakfast served in the rooms is an added treat.

A really outstanding feature of the Prince Solms is Wolfgang's Keller, the restaurant and bar in the basement. Named in honor of German composer Wolfgang Mozart, his portrait has a place of honor in the restaurant. Wolfgang's Keller is presided over by famed pianist Bill McKnight. Bill is not only a maestro at the piano, he is also a maestro in the kitchen. His limited menu has only five items: linguini with clam sauce, a sirloin, a rib eye, chicken provencal, and chicken picatta. The star item is the chicken picatta—boned chicken breasts dipped in seasoned flour and lightly browned in clarified butter and olive oil, then cooked in Madeira. When Marge was re-

Wolfgang's Keller, a restaurant and bar in the basement, features George Washington's favorite dish.

searching our Founding Fathers, she found that this was George Washington's favorite recipe, too, even to the same brand of Madeira.

The brick basement walls of the restaurant are hung with terrific old-fashioned pictures, and dining is by candlelight. Adjacent to the bar is a small sitting area with Victorian sofas and chairs. This romantic atmosphere is enhanced by Bill's beautiful renditions of easy listening music.

For just relaxing, there is the hotel garden and patio. Those enormous stones which make up the floor of the patio area came from

The parlor, like all of the rooms, always has a supply of fresh flowers.

the old Comal County Prison. Each stone was so heavy it was set in place with an overhead crane.

The Prince Solms' manager, Larry Koehler, is a fifth-generation New Braunfels citizen, and makes it his business to preserve the special treatment guests of the inn receive. Breakfast is always freshly-squeezed orange juice and homemade muffins. Every room is filled with fresh fruit and flowers, and the cookie jar is always crammed with cookies. Prince Carl may have preferred his castle at Braunfels, Germany, back in 1845, but then he didn't have the Prince Solms Inn. As this inn offers accommodations fit for a king, surely a mere prince would have found them to his liking.

Stagecoach Inn

Salado, Texas 76571
Phone: 817-947-5111
Accommodations: Restaurant
  only

One of the most historic inns in Texas still stands on the banks of Salado Creek just off Interstate 35, halfway between Dallas and San Antonio. Centuries before the inn was built, the Comanche tribes used this spot as a campground because the mineral springs were a natural attaction for buffalo and other wild game.

When the Spanish arrived, they christened the site Salado, which means "salty," due to minerals in the water. If you like to believe in legends, there are tales of Spanish gold hidden in the cave under the inn that has never been found, and that is supposedly still there.

Such a fine campsite naturally attracted the buffalo hunters in the 1840s, and the first settlers were not far behind. One of the first pioneers to settle in the area, W. B. Armstrong, built the permanent structure in the early 1850s, and it was known as the Shady Villa Hotel.

Stagecoach Inn

Salado became one of the most well-known stops for all the north-south traffic across Texas, and everybody that was anybody stayed at the Shady Villa—good guys and bad guys. Sam Houston made a major anti-secession speech from the hotel's balcony, and right after the Civil War, General George Armstrong Custer signed the register. Salado was a part of the Chisholm Trail, and the cattle kings, Shanghai Pierce and Charles Goodnight, were guests. As Salado was a major stop on the Butterfield Stage line, outlaws Sam Bass, the Daltons, and the James brothers made their presence known. Captain Robert E. Lee, son of the General, was here in pursuit of the infamous Pancho Villa, who was conducting raids into the United States. The priceless register that contained these names and many more was stolen in 1944 and never recovered.

Early in the 1940s the inn was restored by Mr. and Mrs. Dion Van Bibber and named the Stagecoach Inn. Mrs. Van Bibber created the menu which is used today, and the inn is famous for its hush puppies and soup which are served as appetizers. There is very little turnover in personnel among the waitresses, and some have been serving guests for more than 25 years. They still recite the menu, a tradition which started in the old days when whatever was on the stove was that day's fare. The Stagecoach Inn is now owned by Bill Bratten of Los Angeles, but Mr. Van Bibber, now in his nineties, still dines here every evening to make sure the food maintains its flavor and freshness. *Time-Life* Publications selected the Stagecoach Inn as one of the 13 best highway restaurants in the United States.

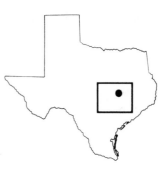

Diversion:

Historic Homes Tour of Salado

The original structure of the Shady Villa Hotel contains only private dining rooms for the restaurant on the ground floor. The upstairs rooms are closed to the public. Still intact are the old floors, beamed ceilings, fireplace, and walls, and these rooms create a charming atmosphere for small parties and gatherings. The main dining rooms are fairly recent additions, but blend in perfectly with the historic part of the building.

Salado, with its old homes and famous Stagecoach Inn, is still one of the most popular stops in Texas. On the lovely tree-shaded grounds is now a modern, well-appointed motel and a large swimming pool. This is an ideal setting for group outings, and vacationers can enjoy fishing, tennis, and golf. The Salado Livery & Company has horse and buggies for rent if you wish to trot around this historic little community. Most of the homes and buildings are marked by the Texas Historical Commission, and the Stagecoach Inn is on the National Register of Historic Places.

The Indians and early settlers knew a good spot when they found one, and the passage of centuries has not changed it one bit. The Stagecoach Inn is no longer just a Texas tradition, it is now a national tradition.

The Gunter Hotel

205 East Houston Street
San Antonio, Texas 78292
Phone: 512-227-3241
Accommodations: 325 rooms, all
*   with bath*
Rates: $50-$55

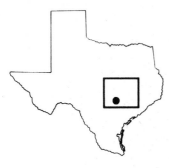

The site on which The Gunter Hotel stands has been used for accommodations for almost 150 years. It was first a stage stop known as the Frontier Inn, and was used by the Vance Brothers Stage and Mail Lines operating between the Mississippi River and Mexico.

The Vance Brothers bought the inn for $500 in 1849 and continued to operate it until the U. S. Army converted it into barracks in 1857. Robert E. Lee was stationed here before assuming command of the Confederate Army, and it was here that orders were signed surrendering U. S. troops in Texas to the Confederacy. After the war, William Tobin leased the site from the Vance Brothers and opened the Vance House Hotel in 1872. By 1877 it had become the best hotel in San Antonio, and prominent citizens moved their apartments here from the Menger.

It became the Mahncke in 1886, and in 1907 L. J. Hart bought the site for under $200,000 and, with the help of the local financier Jot Gunter, began construction of the first steel building in San Antonio. Work was speeded up to beat the opening date of another hotel—the St. Anthony. Built to a height of nine stories, The Gunter cost $565,000. In 1925, T. B. Baker (not of the Dallas Baker Hotel) bought the property, added three more floors, and opened one of the nation's first hotel "coffee shops."

The St. Anthony was where the celebrities stayed, but The Gunter was the cattlemen's hotel. The traditional cattleman's dress was always a black suit, black boots, a white shirt, and a Stetson hat. They came to The Gunter from all parts of the Southwest to make deals, as did politicians. At political conventions and meetings at The Gunter, often stormy and raucous, decisions were made which determined who would hold the positions of power at the courthouse and City Hall, and sometimes in Austin. But The Gunter did have its share of famous guests, and one manager vividly recalls the day Tom Mix rode his horse Tony right into the lobby.

In 1984 San Antonio's historic Gunter Hotel will celebrate her 75th birthday. Her birthday present will be a generous $20+ million

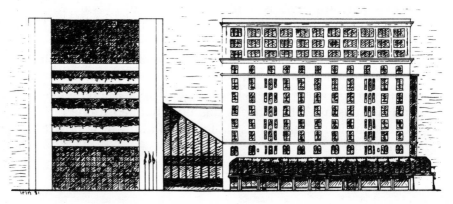

Gunther

renovation. She will get her gift in $10-million allotments. The Gunter Hotel, San Antonio, Inc., a Texas corporation owned largely by Swiss investors, has begun the first stage of enlarging and refurbishing guest rooms and public spaces. This stage is expected to be completed by August 1982.

The second portion of her gift will be a new 12-story building at the corner of St. Mary's and Travis Streets, with the top floor as the Athletic Center and housing a gymnasium, six raquetball courts, a jogging track, and other health club amenities. There will be six floors of parking and two of corporate business suites leased by the year. The rest of the building will be shops, business firms, and restaurants. When the entire project is completed, it will be known as The Gunter Hotel and Athletic Center.

The hotel lobby, into which Tom Mix once rode his horse, Tony.

With the re-design, The Gunter dining rooms will return to their original location on the ground floor of the Houston Street side of the hotel. The front desk, shops, and restaurants will be set in the original 1909 locations in the lobby area. The Cafe Suisse will serve everything from Texas-size hamburgers to filet mignon, and of course, Swiss specialties.

Padre Muldoon's Merrymakin' Libations will be a 250-seat lounge featuring live entertainment in a greenhouse atmosphere. The origin of Padre Muldoon's dates back to the early 19th century when Texas was still under Mexican rule. A prerequisite for land ownership in Texas in those days was conversion to the Roman Catholic faith. Stephen F. Austin agreed to this stipulation, so to fulfill the needs of his 300 settlers, an itinerant priest, Padre Michael Muldoon, occasionally appeared. He was right out of *The Canterbury Tales*, riding a donkey and sipping spirits from an earthenware jug. His fee for baptizing and marrying was usually a refill of his jug. In any case, Padre Muldoon was a great drinking companion. Muldoon, Texas, was named in his honor also, but probably not for the same reasons as The Gunter's lounge.

A new feature of The Gunter will be the Original Old 300 Club, a private club for members, with temporary memberships for hotel guests. It was named for the original 300 settlers who ventured to Texas with Stephen F. Austin. Another new addition will be The Gunter Terrace overlooking Houston and St. Mary's Streets. This impressive glass enclosure will blend modern sophistication with traditional old-style elegance, reminiscent of New Orleans. With its array of old-fashioned lighting effects, hanging plants, and other clusters of foliage, The Gunter Terrace will be an appropriate setting for Sunday brunches, fashion shows, afternoon teas, pre-theater dinners, and after-theater desserts.

All guest rooms will be complete and elegantly refurbished in soft earthtones and vibrant complementary accents. There will be natural hardwood furniture, wildlife paintings, and other luxuries.

The Gunter's birthday present not only assures the future of a great San Antonio landmark, but it is a breakthrough in the revival of the heart of San Antonio. With the rebirth of the nearby Majestic Theater as a center of live entertainment, Houston Street can regain the vigor that made The Gunter corner the accepted hub of San Antonio for decades. But as always with a restoration of this magnitude, the greatest dividend is the rescue of a great historic building.

There have been almost as many famous people at the Menger as there were at the Alamo. Literally across the alley from the Alamo, the Menger began as a two-story stone building erected by William and Mary Menger in 1859. Mary Menger sold the hotel in 1881 to J. H. Kampmann, who was the original builder of the first part of the hotel. Periodically enlarged and remodeled, it became San Antonio's most prominent hotel in the 19th Century.

The Menger's excellent accommodations and meals and its beautiful patio garden attracted such famous guests as General U. S. Grant, General Robert E. Lee, and General John Pershing. Cattle baron Richard King stayed here during the era of the great cattle drives, and poet Sidney Lanier and writer O. Henry signed the register. Theodore Roosevelt recruited his regiment of "Rough Riders" for the Spanish-American War at the Menger in 1898. Also here was Judge Roy Bean's lovely Lillie Langtry, as well as the immortal Sarah Bernhardt. And, of course, President Sam Houston of the Republic of Texas was a frequent guest.

The Menger brought class to Texas and refinement to the frontier. Built as "The finest hotel west of the Mississippi River," the orignal structure has been carefully restored. Old street lamps front the hotel, and dark green grillwork and awnings add to the stark white exterior. In the original wing are rooms and suites furnished with priceless 19th Century antiques. Magnificent four-poster beds, Victorian chairs and sofas upholstered in velvet, marble-top tables, and old-fashioned wallpaper offer the ultimate in guest rooms.

The Rotunda with its gold and white Corinthian columns, massive antique furnishings, two mezzanines with enormous paintings of Western and religious art, and its superb stained glass ceiling is overwhelmingly beautiful. Off of the main lobby, the Rotunda is not in the main stream of hotel traffic, but it is easily one of the most majestic rooms in any Texas bulding and should not be missed.

The patio garden with its lush tropical planting now contains a swimming pool for guests, and the Patio Room Restaurant is open for lunch and dinner. The atmosphere of the restaurant could be described as casual elegance, as could the lobby with one entire wall of glass overlooking the pool and garden.

You can't go to the Menger without going to the famous Menger Bar. With its dark oak paneling on the walls and ceiling, it has a very intimate atmosphere. The back bar is rather unusual with cabinets rather than shelves on each side, and it is complete with brass rail

Menger Hotel and Motor Inn

204 Alamo Plaza
San Antonio, Texas 78205
Phone: 512-223-4361 or 1-800-
* 223-9868*
Accommodations: 196 rooms
* with bath in old section; 103*
* rooms in motor inn*

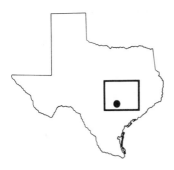

Diversions:

The Alamo
HemisFair Plaza
Institute of Texan Cultures
Missions of San Antonio
The River Walk
La Villita
Spanish Governor's Palace

Menger

and spittoon. Naturally there are lots of pictures of Teddy on the walls, for here is where he recruited his Rough Riders. Not much has changed in the Menger Bar since 1898, and if you close your eyes and listen carefully, you can still hear an occasional "Bully!" echoing around the walls.

Probably no building in San Antonio, except the Alamo itself, has a more glorious past than the Menger. Even though everyone remembers the Alamo, not everyone remembers this grand old hotel. She is still bringing class and refinement to Texas, and a visit to The Shrine of Texas should also include a visit to another monument of Texas history—the Menger.

St. Anthony Hotel

300 East Travis
San Antonio, Texas 78298
Phone: 512-227-4392
*   800-292-5882*
Accommodations: 400 rooms
Rates: $60 +

"Only time can make a hotel this great." Since 1909 time has been making the St. Anthony great. For years, national travel writers have agreed the St. Anthony is one of only three truly distinctive hotels left in the United States among those 50 years or older. (The other two are the Waldorf-Astoria in New York and the Fairmont in San Francisco.)

The St. Anthony was financed and constructed by two prosperous cattlemen named A. H. Jones and B. L. Naylor. In 1936 it was purchased by R. W. Morrison who decided to make the St. Anthony one of the world's most decorous and outstanding hotels. During his world travels, Morrison began buying loads of antiques, paintings, art objects, and hand-woven rugs and bringing them to the hotel. For example, the samovar used in the Peraux Room is a Russian antique that once was the property of Alexander Michailovich and confiscated during the Bolshevik Revolution.

Adjacent to the lobby is the glittering and magnificent Peacock Alley. Added in the thirties, it became known as Peacock Alley be-

cause it was the place where beautiful women came to be seen and admired. Eight crystal chandeliers sparkle over priceless furniture, sculptures, and paintings. The walls are hung with original oils by Remington, Cartier, DeYoung, and McCann. Claud McCann's masterpiece of an eagle is such a focal point and so famous, it is a St. Anthony tradition for people to meet "under the eagle." Chinese urns grace the doorways, and one wall is a grandiose marble fireplace.

Years ago there were twice-daily performances by a string ensemble in Peacock Alley. The pure rosewood piano made for the Russian Embassy in Paris in 1924 and purchased by Morrison for $27,000 in 1936 is still there. Members of the Morin family have been playing this piano since it was brought to the St. Anthony, and Joe Morin is still at the keyboard of this gorgeous antique today. The only time the piano has not been played daily is when Morrison died.

Peacock Alley, added in the thirties, is one of the most beautiful hotel lobbies in the nation.

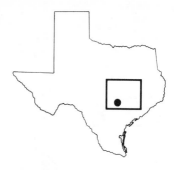

Diversions:

The Alamo
HemisFair Plaza
Institute of Texan Cultures
Missions of San Antonio
The River Walk
La Villita
Spanish Governor's Palace

The St. Anthony was the first hotel in the world to be completely air-conditioned. It was the first to have a drive-in motor and registration entrance where incoming guests could go straight to their rooms without going through the lobby. It was the first hotel to have doors that opened automatically from an electric eye. And the St. Anthony was the first hotel in the country to have a tub and shower in every room. In the 1930s, all of this could be had for $2.50 a day, and no other hotel could offer so much.

The St. Anthony played host to such famous persons as Franklin Roosevelt, Dwight D. Eisenhower, Douglas MacArthur, John Nance Garner, Will Rogers, presidents of Mexico, and numerous other dignitaries. The St. Anthony was *the* hotel for all the celebrities, from the Lone Ranger, Clayton Moore, to the Hollywood premiere of *The Alamo* with its superstar, John Wayne. The Anachaco Room, named for Morrison's ranch, was on the circuit with the Rice, The Adolphus, and the Balinese Room for the big bands—Ted Fiorito, Henry Busey, George Olson, Wayne King, Woody Herman, and Joe Reichman.

The St. Anthony takes pride in The Garden Room, which has been a great place for dinner since the days when Teddy Roosevelt dined here. It serves everything from a leisurely breakfast to a fine dinner in a colorful Spanish atmosphere. There is now a Sunday Brunch from 11:30 a.m. to 2:30 p.m., with champagne, a concert violinist, and informal modeling. There is also the stately Charles V Room (named for Charles V), where diners may savor delicious cocktails and continental cuisine at its finest.

Guest rooms and luxuriously appointed suites are spacious and the epitome of good taste. Handsome and imaginative, each is decorated to have its own unique personality. Accommodations include the popular "double-double" room with two baths.

The hotel boasts that "The St. Anthony is one of a kind. So are you." The staff does go out of its way to make you feel welcome and your visit memorable in this hotel that time has made so great. The special world of the St. Anthony is very special indeed.

Aquarena Springs Inn

Aquarena Springs Exit on I-35
P. O. Box 2330
San Marcos, Texas 78666
Accommodations: 25 rooms, all
  with bath
Rates: $29–$41; suite with
  kitchen $45

Aquarena Springs, the chief tourist attraction in San Marcos, had its beginning back in 1927 when A. B. Rogers—"a rancher, a sportsman, a leading furniture dealer and undertaker, and a progressive citizen"—began to develop the site. He built a golf course and hotel, and later on added glass-bottom boats and an underwater show. The glass-bottom boats were a smash hit, but the hotel was not so fortunate. It has been a hospital and health spa, and for a while it was leased to a school for exceptional children.

Today, Aquarena Springs Inn is one of the most popular places to stay in the Texas Hill Country. This two-story white stucco building

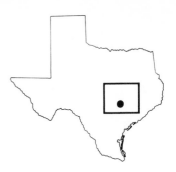

with blue trim resembles something you would expect to see on the Mediterranean Sea, not on the San Marcos River. Built right on the edge of the Aquarena Springs lagoon, the Inn overlooks the diamond clear water of the famous springs. The 19 balcony rooms face the lagoon, and not only do you watch ducks, geese, and swans glide past, but also the glass-bottom boats. The six garden rooms have a view of a tree-clad hillside with a natural aviary.

Impressive as the outside of the building is, the inside was remodeled and re-opened in 1962, and little of the 1927 aura remains. Rooms are like any other modern motel, with contemporary furniture, central heating and air-conditioning, color television, and some kitchenettes. However, the view from the second-story balconies and from the porch that runs the length of the inn provides a real scenic treat.

The commercial attractions surrounding the inn do not detract from its cliff-side setting. Though there is a sky ride, an "authentic" western village, and a Submarine Theater, the inn is off by itself and out of the mainstream of the hundreds of tourists who come to watch the underwater ballet and peer at the fish in the amazingly clear water from the glass-bottom boats.

Diversions:

Swiss sky ride
Underwater ballet in Submarine Theater
Glass-bottom boat rides

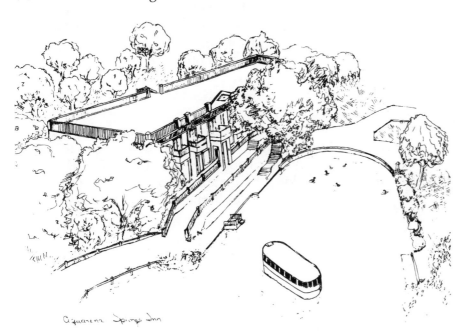

Aquarena Springs Inn

The inn has an olympic-size swimming pool and a beautifully kept golf course. Guests also have access to a nature trail in the Hanging Gardens on the cliff side of the Inn.

The restaurant and lounge is located on the opposite side of the lagoon near the main tourist attractions. It is decorated with a Sea Island motif, and serves good food at moderate prices. One very good selection on the breakfast menu is tacos made with eggs, sausage, and potatoes. The dinner menu contains mostly steak and seafood.

The Springs have been producing millions of gallons of good water every day for centuries. The Tonkawa Indians used the Springs, and later they became a major stop on the Camino Real (the Royal Road, or also known as the Old San Antonio Road)—sort of a 1700s version of today's interstate. The Springs are still a major stop for tourists and vacationers, and the Aquarena Springs Inn is the best place to enjoy their beauty.

Von Minden Hotel

607 Lyons Street
Schulenburg, Texas 78956
Phone: 713-743-3493
Accommodations: 20 rooms with
*   bath; 20 rooms without bath*
Rates: $8–$25
Innkeepers: Bill and Betty Pettit

Back in 1978 a guest's description of the Von Minden was: "You've got to see this hotel. It's built around a movie theater, and if you stay in the hotel you get to go to the movie and eat popcorn free. The sheets are patched and mended, but so clean they squeak. The bathroom has this big tub . . ."

The Von Minden closed shortly afterwards and took on the run-down, neglected look of deserted hotels. The shabby movie sign and the tacky fire escape on the front did not help its appearance, either. Fortunately, two other people loved the Von Minden, and Bill and Betty Pettit purchased it and made its restoration into a family project. They re-opened the hotel in June of 1980 with ten rooms ready for occupancy, and used the original furniture built by the same carpenters who constructed the hotel.

The Von Minden was conceived by Egon Von Minden and built for the convenience of its managers, Irwin Speckels and his wife Leonida Von Minden Speckels. When the hotel opened in 1927, Schulenburg was enjoying the peak of railway transportation, and was a prosperous town. Irwin and Leonida moved into the Von Minden, and a few years later Egon gave it to them. For 52 years, until 1979, the Speckels lived here and raised their two daughters who remember riding their tricycles in the halls on rainy days.

Von Minden

The Cozy Theater, which is also housed in the building, opened in 1926. It was designed for live stage productions as well as for movies, and includes an orchestra pit, dressing rooms, and a beautiful hand-painted canvas curtain advertising businesses of the day. There is even a "crying room" where mothers can take unhappy babies. The movie house re-opened July 4, 1980, with the original seats recushioned. The original sound system still in use is said to be a museum piece. The old projectors are used, also, but with a modern light and film platter system. Bill shows first-run movies and changes the showbill regularly.

The lobby retains the flavor of the twenties, with much of the original furniture.

The Von Minden lobby is much the same as it was in the twenties, small and rather homey with a sitting area, old writing desks, and the original front desk and key racks. One corner has been made into a small gift shop, The Window. It features watercolors of Lucille Gooch, an artist from Kingsville, who not only sells her own paintings, but antiques and collectables as well.

Guest rooms now have ceiling fans, air-conditioning, and color TV. Half of the rooms in the Von Minden have a private bath. However, the "Traveler's Delight," a small single room with a lavatory on the wall and the bath down the hall, can be rented for less than $10. There are no telephones, but if you just tell the desk clerk, you can have ice, coffee, breakfast, or any meal served in your room. The Pettits have put so much work into the rooms, the quarters almost shine from all the care and attention. They are also adding antique pieces to the hotel's original furnishings.

In the rear of the Von Minden is Momma's Pizza Kitchen. Betty Pettit is "Momma," and serves pizza, sandwiches, and a daily lunch special at inexpensive prices. This is one of the most popular spots in Schulenburg, particularly after the movie. Plans are under way for an elegant dining establishment called The Speakeasy to be housed in the Speckels' old apartment.

The trains have quit running, and Interstate 10 bypasses the town, so Schulenburg is mainly a farming community without tourist attractions. There isn't a lot of entertainment in Schulenburg, so the town owes the Pettits a vote of thanks for keeping the Cozy Theater in operation. And people who love old hotels owe the Pettits their undying gratitude for keeping the Von Minden open for guests.

Kyle Hotel

Temple, Texas 76501
Accommodations: 103 room, all
with bath

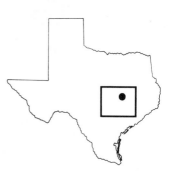

Just looking at the Kyle makes you feel good. Here is an old hotel that has been saved from the fate of so many built in the twenties that were either deserted, made into retirement centers, or torn down completely. The owners of the Kyle believe she should be restored to her original purpose—an elegant hotel.

Temple is a world-famous medical center, and the Kyle was built to house hospital out-patients and visitors. This tallest building in Temple opened in 1929, and in spite of the Depression it was a leading hotel with long lines of people waiting to get rooms. It boasts such well-known guests as Lawrence Welk and his orchestra, Roy Rogers, and Gene Autry. Closed in 1974, work is now in progress to make it once again stand for "the good and gracious things

Kyle Hotel

in life." When it opens in 1982 (write for date), this 13-story super-structure will be the showcase of Central Texas.

Walls have been knocked out between some of the rooms that were hardly larger than a closet, and to make them appear larger, walls and fabrics will be pastel shades. The plastered walls have been re-textured and painted rather than wallpapered as they were in the twenties. Mahogany doors have been stripped of layers of paint and restored to their natural finish along with their hardware. Most of the baths are quite small, but nearly all of the original fixtures will be retained. One of the enlarged baths will have its own jacuzzi. Unfortunately, when air-conditioning was added in the late fifties, 200 Hunter ceiling fans were removed and lost forever. The remodeled Kyle will have no "standard hotel rooms," and all will be decorated on an individual basis.

Heavy beamed ceilings and a massive wrought-iron chandelier give the lobby a Spanish effect. Two cast-stone columns have a most unusual bas-relief at the top. Instead of the traditional capital decorated with acanthus leaves, they have a woman's face and a man's face with a tremendous handle-bar moustache and a bald head. Each face is repeated several times on each column. You can't help but wonder why the unknown sculptor chose these particular faces for the decoration.

The hotel will be left intact as much as possible, but the roof of the ground floor dining room will be raised about 10 feet to install windows to let in natural light and create a feeling of more space. On one side of the hotel entrance will be the coffee shop, and on the opposite side will be a ground-level lounge and club. Both will have entrances from inside the hotel and from the street to attract patrons that are not staying in the hotel.

The thirteenth floor will be a private club with an ultra-plush decor. The extremely high ceilings will be lined with mirrors, and the walls upholstered in fabric. The original Mexican tile floor will be buffed and polished to restore its vivid colors. The varying shades of blue within each floor tile were set individually, making the floor irreplaceable today. This penthouse area also has an outdoor terrace which will be open to club members.

The Kyle's exterior will be almost as it was in 1929, except every window had to be replaced. The arches and wrought-iron lights over the three entrances will remain, but another fire escape had to be added to the east side of the hotel. The front sidewalk will be removed to allow installation of planters and a half-circle drive, as the owners plan to offer valet parking for guests.

With all this and much more in store for her, the Kyle will take her place among the real first-class hotels in Texas. From grand old to grand new, the Kyle will once again be synonymous with elegance.

Weimar Country Inn

Jackson Square
Weimar, Texas 78962
Accommodations: 9 rooms, 8
baths

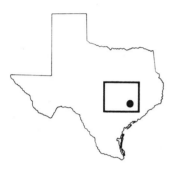

Without the old Galveston, Harrisburg, and San Antonio Railway there never would have been a Weimar, Texas. A railroad builder and one of the town's founders, T. W. Peirce, had once visited the town of Weimar, Germany, and was so favorably impressed with it that he desired to name one of the towns along the railroad after this beautiful German city. Unlike Fredericksburg and New Braunfels, Weimar did not even have any German citizens when it was founded in 1873. Though there are now quite a few German names in Weimar, the German citizens did not arrive until much later.

Naturally a railroad town has to have a hotel, so in 1909 the San Jacinto Hotel was built on the site of two previous Jackson Hotels. It operated under a succession of owners until July of 1970, when it became the property of the City of Weimar. It was slated for demolition until a group of businessmen decided to form a corporation and save her. Ron Jones of Houston is in charge of the restoration. It's always interesting to know the reasons why people decide to take on the myriad problems of restoring an old building, and Ron's were, "I love property, and I love old things. I also wanted a place near my ranch in Weimar to go out to dinner and enjoy an evening." The Weimar Country Inn, due to open in 1982 (write for date), will have all those amenities and more.

Weimar Country Inn

There wasn't much left of the old frame building when Jones' group took it over. The claw-foot tubs had been sold, and the doors and wainscoting had gone to restoration projects in Round Top. The interior had been gutted, and the only thing left was a pile of old sinks heaped in a corner.

Back in the thirties the hotel was "modernized," and records are not clear as to just what that involved. But the eighties will see big changes.

A stucco covering has been removed from the outside, and the exterior will be the original frame structure. Walls have been torn out inside to enlarge the small guest rooms. All will be wallpapered, ceiling fans will be installed, and rooms will be furnished in antiques. Modern plumbing, and central heating and air-conditioning will be installed.

The inn will have a main dining room, a garden room, and the Cowboy Lounge. Country cooking, steaks, and barbeque are planned as the bill of fare.

It is always exciting to find an old building being restored, particularly to its original purpose, and the Weimar Country Inn shows promise as becoming one of the best inns in Texas.

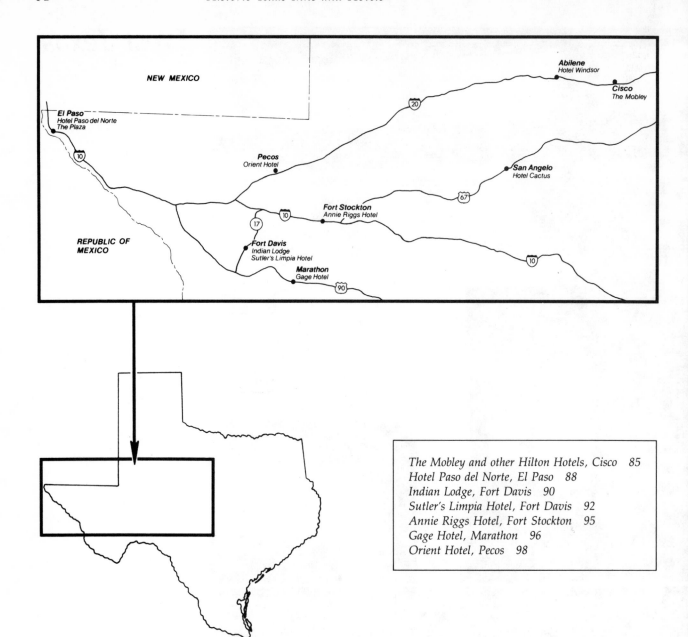

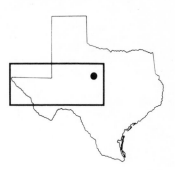

When Conrad Hilton decided to make his fortune in Texas back in 1919, he arrived from New Mexico with $5000 and the determination to buy a bank. His first defeat was in Wichita Falls, where the bank was not interested in selling to anyone. Everyone else in Texas seemed to be getting rich off the oil boom around Ranger, so Hilton headed for the bank in Cisco. To his chagrin, the bank in Cisco wasn't for sale either. Discouraged, Hilton decided to get a night's rest and plan his next move.

As Hilton headed for the Mobley Hotel, it was merely a convenient place to sleep, and nothing more. He found he wasn't the only one in Cisco trying to get a bed, for the lobby was packed. He was told to come back in eight hours when there would be a turnover of beds, as there just might be a place to sleep. A hard-faced gentleman began pushing him out of the hotel with the admonition that loitering wasn't allowed in the lobby. About to explode with anger, Hilton was suddenly curious. "You mean you rent beds for eight hours and then get a complete turnover?" That question was the most momentous one of Hilton's life. The unpleasant gentleman turned out to be Mobley, who was resentful of his hotel business that kept him from making a fortune in the oil fields. Mobley was renting rooms three times in a 24-hour period, and Hilton couldn't believe he really wanted to sell a sure thing to take his chances in oil speculation. When Hilton offered to meet Mobley's price for his hotel, one of the greatest success stories of all times began.

After using the Mobley as his training ground, Hilton began to look around for other hotel investments. He went on to the Terminal and the Melba in Fort Worth, then his first Waldorf in Dallas, and the Beaton in Corsicana. Finally, tired of face-lifting run-down properties, he decided to build a Hilton Hotel. At Main and Harwood in Dallas, on July 26, 1924, Conrad Hilton spaded up a bit of earth and threw it over his shoulder, thus breaking ground for the first hotel with his own name on it.

Of course, one Hilton Hotel would not be enough. There had to be one in Abilene, Waco, Marlin, Plainview, San Angelo, Lubbock, and El Paso. His dream of Texas "wearing a chain of Hilton hotels" came true. But terrible years for the hotel industry were looming on the horizon. The time was the early thirties, and Hilton lost them all.

Mobley Hotel

A lesser man than Conrad Hilton might have given in to despair, but he had become a dedicated hotel man. Slowly Hilton began to recoup his losses and even regained several of his original hotels. The rest is history—a history that had its beginning in Cisco, Texas. What has happened to all of those original Hiltons? Well, the Mobley is still there in Cisco today. Square, red, and ugly, it is hard to envision this old building as the beginning of the most famous chain of hotels in the world. The hotel and the funds to restore it as a museum have been donated by the Hilton Corporation to the Conrad Hilton Hotel and Restaurant Management School at the University of Houston. The Lubbock Hilton has been torn down, and the Plainview Hilton is now a run-down, low-rent apartment building. At least it is called the Hilton Apartments. As for the rest, they are still in operation in one form or another.

Hotel Windsor

4th & Pine
Abilene, Texas 79604
Phone: 915-672-3261
Accommodations: 30 rooms with
*   bath; 40 apartments*
Rates: $24–$26

Hilton built the Abilene Hilton in 1927, and it was considered one of the finest hotels of that era. Today the Hotel Windsor is a large, yellow brick edifice that obviously has seen more glorious days. The lobby is quite bare with only a few pieces of pseudo-Spanish furniture. Rooms look rather like a present day Hilton hotel. They are just standard hotel rooms with color TV, wall-to-wall carpeting, and air-conditioning.

The restaurant's blue and white lattice decor is quite pleasing, and the food is good. Open only for breakfast and lunch six days a week and for a buffet on Sunday, the menu is rather limited, and all meals are inexpensive. Overall, Hotel Windsor has all the earmarks of the retirement hotel that it predominately is.

During the hard times of the thirties, a band leader came through and offered to play here just for room and board for a few days. He was a roaring success and ended up staying several months. Abilene just adored Lawrence Welk.

The Plaza

Main and Harwood
Dallas, Texas
Phone: 214-742-7251
Accommodations: 286 rooms
*   with bath*
Rates: $35–$50

The very first hotel to bear the Hilton name is still very much in operation today. Built in 1925, only the outside remains unchanged. Very little is left of the interior except some of the mahogany paneling and Williamsburg chandeliers. The large brass mailbox is the one installed in 1925, and the huge urn was found in the basement. Described as a "pleasant, clean, and safe medium-priced hotel in the heart of downtown Dallas," the Plaza is a real "find."

The Plaza

Oregon and Mills Streets
El Paso, Texas 79901
Phone: 915-532-5661
Accommodations: 150 rooms
*   with bath*
Rates: $30–$36

Two ex-Hilton hotels have the same name, but they are not part of a chain, nor do they have the same owner. In old downtown El Paso, the Plaza still has the famous Hilton crest on the bronze elevator doors. Even the blankets, shower doors, and rugs bearing his trademark are still in use. The lobby is unimpressive now, but the rooms are in fairly good condition. Rates are extremely reasonable for such an ideal location. Unlike the rest of the Hiltons, built of yellow brick, the El Paso Hilton is constructed of the dull red variety.

This was Hilton's last hotel before he went broke in the thirties.

This little Central Texas town is blessed with the world's deepest and strongest mineral-water wells, flowing more than 380,000 thermal gallons daily. Discovered in 1892, the medicinal possibilities of the water were soon realized, and Marlin became a resort and spa "boomtown." Thousands of visitors came here to "take the baths," and when Hilton opened his hotel on May 27, 1930, attending the opening were Huey P. Long, governor of Louisiana, and the governors of four other states.

Hilton built an underground tunnel from the hotel to the Marlin Sanitarium Bathhouse across the street. Guests clad in pajamas and robes had convenient access to the baths. As many as 350 bathers a day were soaked, salved, and massaged. The bathhouse is still there, but now closed, and neglect has set in. Marlin has put her "miracle waters" to more practical uses such as heating the hospital and the Chamber of Commerce using geothermal energy.

The hotel became The Falls in 1968, and several floors have now been converted to apartments. All other guest rooms are freshly painted, with new carpeting, cable TV, and telephones. The hotel's El Domingo restaurant serves an inexpensive, delicious buffet every day of such fare as roast beef, meat loaf, and smothered steak.

The Falls

226 Coleman
Marlin, Texas 76661
Phone: 817-883-2511
Accommodations: 40 rooms with
  bath
Rates: $21–$30

Built in 1929, the Hotel Cactus still has the Hilton crest on the front of the building, but it has been a retirement center since 1963. The lobby is still lovely, with Spanish tiles around the walls, on the columns, and on the steps leading to the mezzanine. Ornate cast-iron and brass fixtures still hang from the paneled ceiling. The entire building has been preserved in excellent condition and has retained a great deal of its original grandeur. The whole place bustles with activities for its senior citizens.

Hotel Cactus

902 North Main
San Angelo, Texas
Phone: 915-655-7391

The Regis was one of Hilton's first hotels, and it opened July 3, 1928. After Hilton lost it during the Depression, it was acquired by a local group of speculators who changed it to the Roosevelt. After many years as a business and social success, it, too, began to go down hill. One of the owners, A. V. McDonnell, took it over and donated it to the Catholic diocese. They converted it to the present Regis Retirement Center, now splendidly run and "full up." Some years ago they added to it St. Elizabeth's Hospital. This retirement and convalescent home is now considered to be one of the finest in Texas.

The gigantic Hilton Corporation today is no longer interested in these archaic little properties and has made no effort to acknowledge them in any way. Only The Falls in Marlin has a historical marker to the fact that it was one of the original links in Hilton's dream of Texas "wearing a chain of Hilton hotels." Well, Texas has

The Regis

400 Austin Avenue
Waco, Texas 76703
Telephone: 817-756-5441

more than enough Hiltons today to realize Conrad's dream a hundred times over, but they all had their beginning a long time ago in tiny Cisco, Texas, and later at Main and Harwood in Dallas. Fortunately the Mobley is slated for preservation, but the rest will be unacknowledged stepping stones to one of the world's greatest fortunes.

Hotel Paso del Norte

115 S. El Paso Street
El Paso, Texas 79901
Telephone: 915-533-2421
Accommodations: 191 rooms
with bath

From bullet holes in the tenth-story windows fired during Pancho Villa days, to a plaque on the corner describing El Paso's infamous gunfights in 1881, the Hotel Paso del Norte rises! This majestic lady formally opened her doors with a lavish ball on Thanksgiving night in 1912, and was hailed as the "showplace of the West." Her history is as grand as she is.

On February 11, 1892, El Paso's Grand Hotel was totally destroyed by fire. Occupants jumped from the third- and fourth-story windows while the town hopelessly tried to extinguish the blaze. One of those who helped was Zach T. White, who had made a fortune in hardware and bricks. He always cited this incident as the start of his idea to build a fireproof hotel in El Paso.

Later, in April of 1906, when San Francisco was in ruins from that historic earthquake, Zach White had an engineer copy the design of those buildings still standing. These plans, along with a fireproof design, materialized as the Hotel Paso del Norte (the Hotel on the Pass to the North). Built at a cost of $1.5 million, a major expense was hauling the white gypsum for the fireproof walls from nearby White Sands, New Mexico.

White always referred to the hotel as his "dream hotel," and when his dream became a reality, no detail was spared in its construction. When you enter the lobby and walk under the magnificent antique Tiffany stained glass dome, you enter a different world. The dome is so breathtakingly beautiful, you almost miss the elaborate mahogany carvings, walls with cherrystone, golden scagliola and black serpentine marble, and the European chandeliers. And there are still some of the original mahogany and Russian walnut furniture that White imported from Europe.

In the past, the Paso del Norte has seen much notable activity. During the Mexican revolution, only a few years after the hotel's construction, El Pasoans and members of the press watched the skirmishes in Juarez from the upper floors. Among the famous guests have been Mexican presidents Obregon and Diaz, and U. S. Presidents Taft and Hoover, and Nixon when he was Vice President. Following the signing of the Chamizal Treaty in 1968, Presidents Lyndon Johnson and Diaz Ordaz dined at a luncheon held in the hotel lobby. Other well-known visitors were Pancho Villa, Gloria

Hotel Paso del Norte

Swanson, Will Rogers, General Pershing, Eleanor Roosevelt, Caruso, Charles Lindbergh, and Amelia Earhart. The Paso del Norte was even the setting for two mysteries, Don Hamilton's *The Wrecking Crew* and Erle Stanley Gardner's *The Case of the Careless Cupid*.

From the very beginning, the hotel has been a center of cattle trading. The Paso del Norte claims that more head of cattle have been bought or sold in its lobby than at any other single location in the world. There is even the story of one of the guests who was discovered to be a thief robbing other hotels, but not the Paso del Norte. When questioned, the thief replied that because of the friendly atmosphere, the courteous service, and the good food, he could not rob his "home."

Big things are in store for the hotel. It is undergoing extensive remodeling, and plans are to re-open the hotel in 1982 (write for date). Placed on the National Register of Historic Places, it will be restored to its former splendor. The beautiful lobby, fashioned by Italian artisans and highlighted by the magnificent Tiffany dome, will remain essentially unchanged. The Ben Dowell Saloon, named for El Paso's first mayor and saloon keeper, will be reworked to flow with the lobby, and the Parlor Car Bar and Union Depot Restaurant will be completely renovated into one gracious dining room renamed the Tiffany Room. The lobby's six original columns and their decorative sculpting, now covered by a false ceiling, will be exposed, and the archway between the dining room and the lobby will be opened. The Wrangler Room with its famous mural "Pass to the North" will be retained. Elevators will be restyled, but will continue to be manual with elevator operators. There are many more

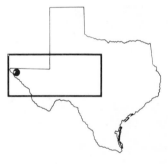

Diversions:

Aerial Tramway to Ranger Peak
Chamizal National Memorial
El Paso Museum of Art
Fort Bliss
Juarez, Mexico
Scenic drives
Tigua Indian Reservation

mechanical and back-of-the-house changes, but every effort is being made to preserve the traditional charm.

Overall, the Paso del Norte will be more beautiful than ever. Zack White's "dream hotel" will be beyond his wildest fancies, and she will once again take her place as "the showplace of the West."

Indian Lodge

P. O. Box 786
Fort Davis, Texas 79734
Phone: 915-426-3254
Accommodations: 39 rooms, all
*   with bath*
Rates: $16 +

To get to the Davis Mountains, you have to face the barren wastes, the tumbling tumbleweeds, the endless horizons, and all the other dreary features that make a desert. For no matter which direction you travel, the landscape is nothing but scrub, with only an occasional buzzard gliding overhead to break the monotony. One early pioneer described the area as "maddening to the brain." This is the land that people elsewhere see in their mind's eye when they picture Texas. This is the Texas of the western novels and movies. But once you finally approach the Davis Mountains, you enter a different world entirely.

These mountains are not as rugged as the Guadalupe Mountains or the ones in Big Bend, but they are an oasis of beauty in this desolation. Trees, lush vegetation, pristine streams, and mountain scenery combine to make this one of the loveliest areas not only in Texas but in the Southwest. There is no question as to the quality of the air out here, either, for it is so perfect and clear that Mt. Locke was chosen as the site of McDonald Observatory. Literally, on a clear night you can see forever, and you don't even have to be aided by a telescope.

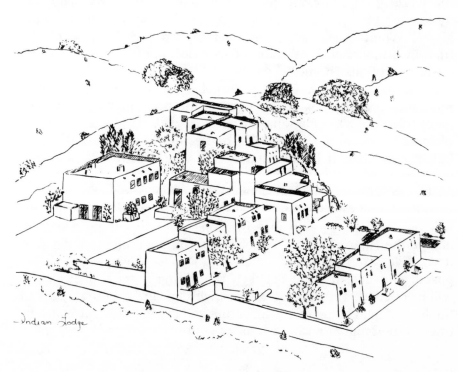
Indian Lodge

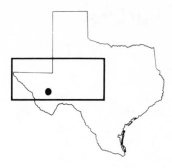

There is no need to rough it at Davis Mountains State Park. Incredibly enough, here in this isolated park is one of the best hotels and restaurants in the entire state—Indian Lodge. This pueblo-style adobe structure was built in the 1930s when only government agencies were doing any kind of construction. In 1933, the Civilian Conservation Corps built this lodge so well that it looks brand new today, both inside and out.

Adobe is a traditional construction material in the Southwest. Not only is adobe a sun-dried mud brick, adobe is the earth from which the brick is formed, and it is also the structure made of the brick. The horrendous desert heat and the cold nights seldom penetrate its natural insulation. Indian Lodge's walls are more than 18 inches thick in places, and it is considered one of the outstanding adobe buildings in the state. Be that as it may, Indian Lodge is still air-conditioned and has fireplaces in each room, although fires are no longer allowed.

The furnishings in the Lodge are right in keeping with its architecture and surroundings. Many of the cedar beds, dressers, chests, and tables were made by the CCC workers when they built the lodge. Of fairly basic design, most of the pieces are so heavy they are very difficult to move. Carpets and curtains are in an Indian design, and walls are bare as were the Indian pueblo dwellings. All rooms face east and have a view of the gorgeous sunrise over the Davis Mountains.

The lobby has the same massive furniture, bare wood floors, a fireplace at each end, and heavy tree-trunk columns supporting a beamed ceiling. The lobby is rarely used, for there are several verandas which guests prefer because of their natural beauty. All are landscaped with buckhorn cactus, yucca plants, prickly pears, ocotillos, and cedar that blend harmoniously with the Lodge's white stucco that covers the adobe construction. A large heated pool completes the picture of a perfect desert retreat.

The dining room serves such good food that campers and local residents often jam it, making service somewhat slow. Prices are reasonable, and the menu extensive. Not only are there steaks, but also lobster tails, king crab legs, Mexican food, and special dinner items such as liver and onions. Alcoholic beverages are not served, nor are they allowed in the public areas.

Indian Lodge is closed the first two weeks in January for repairs and renovation, but open the rest of the year. Reservations are a must, particularly on weekends and holidays, but they can be made a year in advance.

You may think you are a zillion miles from nowhere as you head for the Davis Mountains State Park, but when you get to the sign advising that you are on the "Highest Road East of the Rockies," you know it's a part of Texas that is truly worth the effort of getting there.

Diversions:

Davis Mountains State Park
  scenic drive
Fort Davis National Historic
  Site with sound re-creation of
  a military retreat parade from
  the 1800s
Overland Trail Museum
Scenic drive—a 74-mile loop on
  Texas 166 and Texas 17
McDonald Observatory

Sutler's Limpia Hotel

P. O. Box 822
Fort Davis, Texas 79734
Phone: 915-426-3237
Accommodations: 9 rooms, 2
* suites, all with bath*
Rates: $27+
Innkeeper: J. C. Duncan

Several momentous events made Fort Davis a key post in the defense system of West Texas. After Texas joined the Union and the Mexican War was over, gold was discovered in California in 1849. Intent upon avoiding the winter snows and rugged mountains of the central routes to the gold fields, thousands of immigrants made their way over the southern trails. A vital segment of the route was the San Antonio-El Paso road. Indian warpaths into Mexico intersected the El Paso road, and by 1854, Comanche and Apache depredations had grown to such alarming proportions that a fort became essential to protect immigrants, settlers, and the famed Butterfield Overland Mail that used the road.

A pleasant box canyon near Limpia Creek was selected as the site, and the new fort was named for then Secretary of War, Jefferson Davis. From 1854 to 1860 little real progress was made in solving the Indian problem. For a few years camels were tested successfully for use on American deserts at Ft. Davis, but then the Civil War destroyed the entire frontier defense system. The camels were turned loose in the desert, and for many years scared the daylights out of wandering prospectors. Fort Davis was occupied by Confederate troops for nearly a year, but soldiers were needed to fight Yankees, not Indians, so the fort was abandoned and later wrecked by the Apaches. In 1867 the Union forces returned, and Fort Davis was the first post in the west to receive black soldiers. These "Buffalo Soldiers," as they were called by the Indians, compiled a notable record of military accomplishments. With the surrender of Geronimo in 1886, the Apache wars came to an end, and so did Fort Davis.

Sutler's Limpia Hotel

The army withdrew from the fort, but the town did not die. In fact, it began to attract a great number of tourists and enjoyed a boom as a health resort because of its invigorating climate. In 1912 a group of local merchants formed the Union Trading Company and built a 12-room hotel out of pink limestone quarried near the town. The hotel was named for nearby Limpia Creek, which means "clear" in Spanish, but for some reason the owners misspelled the name, and it was christened "The Lympia."

The hotel must have been the last word in elegance with its metal ceilings with rounded corners, its gaslights powered by its own carbide plant, and its turn-of-the-century oak furniture. There was a

12-room addition in 1920, so it obviously was a favorite of its visitors.

Later, the Lympia served as offices, a variety of businesses, and then apartments. In 1972, J. C. Duncan, who had owned the building in the 1950s, purchased it again. As a teacher and superintendent of schools, he was dismayed at the apathy of the town towards its rich and colorful history. The State of Texas had begun restoration of the fort, but the town itself was in dire need of repair. Duncan had the novel idea of having his government class construct models of the square as it looked in the early 1900s. These 20 students attacked their project with a vengence, and this was the impetus the town needed. The Fort Davis State Bank has been restored, homes have become little showplaces, and even businesses without historical value look prosperous and cared for.

The Limpia has been refurnished with new carpeting, wallpaper, and furniture.

Duncan has the hotel open once again under the name of Sutler's Limpia Hotel. He changed the hotel's name for two reasons. As a teacher he could not bear to retain the original misspelled Lympia, and second, a sutler was important to the old military forts. It was at the sutler's store that the soldier supplied himself with goods that made his drab life in this lonely post more bearable. The sutler was "bound to keep on hand" items other than the few necessities provided by the Army. As to be expected, not all of the sutlers were honest, and the Congress in 1866 voted not to renew their privileges.

The Limpia certainly has "on hand" all the comforts of today's society. It looks much as it did in the twenties, except bathrooms, air-conditioning, and television have been added. The lobby, or parlor, is carpeted in an Axminster reproduction and wallpapered in a tiny floral design so dear to the heart of Victorian decorators. Overstuffed velvet chairs and Victorian light fixtures enhance the decor. The oak front desk has stained-glass panels, and its door is from the Duncan ranch home built in 1894.

Upstairs guest rooms still have transoms, metal ceilings with rounded corners, and oaken furniture. Heating and air-conditioning units have been cleverly hidden by cornice boards. All rooms have matching blue bedspreads and curtains of a cottage eyelet design.

A second-floor veranda was added to the Limpia and offers a nice view of the county's 1910 courthouse, but the best spot in the hotel is the glassed-in sunporch next to the main parlor. Amply furnished with rattan rocking chairs, the sunporch is the favorite gathering place of the hotel's guests.

The sunporch provides a cheery gathering place for hotel guests.

Also "on hand" are the Sutler's Store and The Boarding House Restaurant. The old cavalry soldier couldn't use a thing in the store today, for it is now a very modern gift shop. More suited to his needs is the private club at The Boarding House. Hotel guests automatically get a free guest card, whereas temporary memberships are $2.00 for those not staying at the Limpia. The restaurant serves good country dinners, salads, sandwiches, and a noon buffet, all at moderate prices. The souvenir menu gives the history of the Limpia and an explanation of the sutlers.

Thanks to a dedicated teacher and hard-working students and citizens, Fort Davis is once again the place heat-weary Texans and others from all parts of the world come to visit. There is no richer gift to leave to the present than a restoration of part of the past.

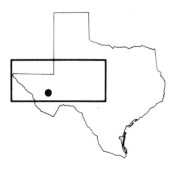

Diversions:

McDonald Observatory
Fort Davis National Historic
  Site
Scenic loop drive, Highways
  118 and 166
Davis Mountains State Park
Overland Trail Museum

The army established Fort Stockton in 1859 to keep the raiding Comanches out of Mexico as part of the Guadalupe-Hidalgo treaty, and also to protect travelers using the Old Spanish Trail to California. The site had long been famous as Comanche Springs long before it ever became a fort. These springs originally flowed 60 million gallons of water per day, and were an important stop on the Comanche War Trail. As early as 1534, Cabeza de Vaca found the fabulous springs as he wandered around the Southwest trying to get back to Mexico.

Fort Stockton became a major post for the army, but with the arrival of the railroad the fort was doomed. The army withdrew in 1886, but the town had become such an important stop, its future was secure. In 1899, six men finally completed their five-year task of building a hotel. In 1902 Mrs. Annie Riggs took over the hotel, and it became a "hanging out place" for early-day politicians, cowboys, and ranch families. Mrs. Riggs was a soft-spoken, cultured and refined lady who ran a first-class establishment.

Fort Stockton has 15 medallions awarded to its historical sites, and particularly worthy of its medallion is the Annie Riggs Hotel. The building is one of the finest examples of an adobe structure in Texas. It was the pride of the West when it was built, and today it is one of the best pioneer museums in the state. The rooms have been converted into showcases of old western memorabilia. The Cowboy Room features the gear of Fort Stockton's tallest cowboy, seven-foot Frank Hinde. The kitchen is in such good condition that the 1910 electric stove still works. A mysterious bullet hole is in the wall of one of the rooms, and no one knows why it is there. In addition to its handsome furnishings, the parlor contains two old, very rare bibles. On the wall of the old lobby is a wonderful handmade quilt stitched in cattle brands used in Pecos County from 1875 to 1910, with 192 different squares.

One of the most interesting exhibits in the museum is an old rolltop desk which belonged to the infamous Sheriff Royal who ruled Pecos County with six notches on his gun. From 1855 to 1894, he struck such fear in the people they became desperate to be rid of him. In a secret meeting in November 1894, six of the leading citizens met and drew for the black bean to see who would murder

Annie Riggs Hotel

301 South Main Street
Fort Stockton, Texas 79735
Accommodations: Museum only
Hours: Open daily except
*   Wednesday*
Admission: 50 cents

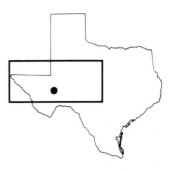

Diversions:

Fort Stockton Historical Tour
Dinosaur Tracks, U.S. 67
Pisanso Pete, a 12-foot high
*   fiberglass chaparral, Ft.*
*   Stockton's symbol of the Great*
*   Southwest*

Annie Riggs Hotel

the sheriff. Shortly thereafter, Sheriff Royal was shot with a shotgun while seated at this desk. His murder was never solved, and his tombstone bearing the inscription "Assassinated" is still in the old fort cemetery. This cemetery is a testimonial to the hardships of frontier life, as no headstone shows the age of any person to be over 40.

There are many other fine exhibits in this great little museum, including a geological display, for today Fort Stockton is a big oil and gas center. Comanche Springs is now a swimming pool, and the railroad has been replaced by Interstate 10; but if Mrs. Annie Riggs could see her hotel now, she would no doubt heartily approve of the "cultured and refined" way it is being used.

Gage Hotel

Highway 90
Marathon, Texas 79842
Phone: 915-386-4560
Accommodations: 19 rooms, 7
* baths*
Rates: $30–$40

Brewster County is the largest county in Texas, even larger than the state of Connecticut, but it only has the two towns of Alpine and tiny Marathon. Marathon was named by a sea captain who said it reminded him of the area around Marathon, Greece. In the good old days of the railroad, Marathon was a bustling ranching and mining center. It even had a rather unusual rubber factory. Rubber can actually be produced from the bark of the guayule, a gray desert shrub that grows profusely in this part of Texas. However, the bushes did not produce much rubber, nor did they grow back after they were cut, so the rubber industry was not very profitable. Abandoned in 1926, the factory had a brief revival during World War II, but the invention of synthetic rubber ended Marathon's industry forever.

Back in the twenties, a wealthy rancher, banker, and San Antonio businessman famous for his shrewd business acumen had big plans for Marathon. Alfred Gage owned 500,000 acres of ranch land near

Gage Hotel

here and made frequent trips to these vast holdings. Since there was no hotel in the entire area, Alfred decided to build his own which would also serve as his headquarters.

In 1927 the Gage Hotel opened its doors, and it was hailed as "modern in every respect." It must have truly been an oasis in this sparsely populated land. For even today, this part of Texas has the kind of scenery that makes you avidly look forward to the historical markers and marvel that anything at all ever occurred here. Nevertheless, the Gage quickly became a famous and popular watering hole in this inhospitable land. Unfortunately, Alfred was not to enjoy his hotel's success, for he died a year after it was completed. As so often happens, with the passage of years the Gage fell into a sad state of disrepair.

Now once again the Gage is an oasis—in fact, one of the finest west of the Pecos. This time its benefactor is J. P. Bryan, Jr., also a rancher who wanted modern accommodations when he came to his ranch near Marathon. This present-day Alfred Gage has taken the old hotel and restored it to a state that would have thoroughly pleased its builder. Alfred would certainly approve of the additions of air-conditioning, new plumbing, and a swimming pool.

This sturdy yellow-brick structure was completely sound even after years of neglect. Removal of the hideous linoleum and a treatment of linseed oil and turpentine revealed pine floors in excellent condition. After application of 130 gallons of paint stripper to remove six varying coats of paint, the woodwork is once again its natural finish. Walls have been replastered and repainted and all 55 windows rescreened. After all, there are many days in this arid climate that you will prefer Marathon's clean fresh air to air-conditioning.

Persimmon Gap, Stillwell's Crossing, Black Gap, Dead Horse, Santiago Peak, and The Chalk are not only sites in Brewster County, they are also the names of the Gage's downstairs guest rooms. The furnishings are right in keeping with the hotel, with an 1840 German pine bed and an 1860 four-poster. All rooms have a ceiling fan and a wash basin. A few rooms share a bath, but the most modern conveniences are just a few steps down the hall.

The lobby still has the original front desk and key box, but the old mailboxes were taken from the post office in Alpine when it used to be known as Murphysville. For some reason the lobby fireplace was a fake one and could never be used, and it is still that way now. On one wall is a magnificent antique cabinet that looks as though it came from a Spanish hacienda, but actually it came from the Gage Inn in England. Just off the lobby is the wash room just as it functioned in 1927. That is all it was—a wash room—with nothing in it but a wash basin. The wooden telephone booth in the corner is a copy of the one that has long since been removed and lost.

The dining room's emphasis is on traditional fare. It features huge steaks, hamburgers, lamb chops, broiled quail, and a special grilled

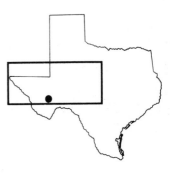

Diversions:

Gateway to Big Bend National Park

Black Gap Wildlife Management Area

Great Marathon Basin, a rockhound's paradise

Stillwell's Crossing, named for an actual location in Brewster County, is decorated in authentic period furniture.

cheese sandwich with bacon and jalapeños. Breakfast will offer sour dough biscuits, and the lunch menu will be the same as the dinner menu. A small bar called the Watering Trough is in the basement.

The Gage is a perfect overnight or weekend stopover. Whether you are just traveling through or on your way to Big Bend, when you reach Marathon you will be mighty grateful to Alfred Gage and J. P. Bryan, Jr., for making this welcome little oasis possible.

Orient Hotel

U. S. Highway 285
Pecos, Texas 79772
Accommodations: West of the
* Pecos Museum*
Hours: Mon.–Sat. 9 a.m.–
* 6 p.m.; Sun. 2 p.m.–6 p.m.*
Admission: 50 cents

West of the Pecos—a phrase with the sound of a Hollywood western and this part of Texas—has enough history and legends to produce a library of movie scripts. This arid country of scrubby deserts was the last frontier in settling the west, and only the arrival of the railroad tamed the land and its inhabitants.

Pecos, named for the river that meanders through West Texas, came into existence as did so many towns in the West. It was founded in 1881 as a way station on the Texas & Pacific Railroad. In 1896, R. S. Johnson, a former Texas Ranger, bought a lot at First and Cedar Streets and built a two-story red sandstone building. The stone was quarried just east of Barstow, and it was this quarry that supplied the material for many Texas buildings. The lower floor became the "Number 11 Saloon." Here the cowboys came to get drunk on their trips to town.

In October of 1896 there occurred a double killing in the Number 11. Barney Riggs, the bartender, killed Bill Earhart and John Denson. These men had threatened to kill him, and he met their dare. Bronze markers have been placed in the saloon floor showing where the two men fell.

In 1904 Johnson decided to enlarge the Orient's hotel facilities. Furniture was brought in from Chicago, and each room had a big rug, an iron bed, two chairs, and a washstand. Each floor had one large, complete bathroom. The lobby was not highly decorated, but just met the needs of a frontier town that had no paved sidewalks nor even graveled streets, just dust or mud. The lobby is now furnished very much as it was in 1904, and the carbide gas lights are still there.

The hotel owned a big black bus, which was drawn by two large white horses with a Negro attendant driving. The T & P depot was on the north side of the tracks, and because of the dust and mud, the bus met all trains and delivered passengers to the hotel and also took them back to the trains. The saloon was closed when the hotel opened, and was replaced by a pool room. At that time women were welcome, and they played pool or billiards along with the men.

The demise of the railroad brought about the demise of the Orient. When the City of Pecos purchased the building in 1963, it needed tremendous repair and renovation. Organizations and individuals raised funds and donated their time. Various groups requested certain rooms for refurbishing, but all requests had to be approved by a Museum Board. The Board believes that every person in the town of Pecos and many others from surrounding counties gave either cash, time, or both to creating this outstanding little museum.

When the Museum Board took over the hotel's renovation, the woodwork was covered with coats and coats of various colors of paint. After volunteer workers applied many gallons of paint remover, beautiful natural wood was uncovered. Original newel posts were found in a junk room, and the sign advertising the rooms up-

Orient Hotel

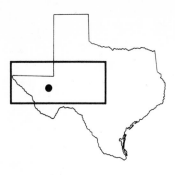

Diversions:

Gateway to Carlsbad Caverns
Toyah, a rockhound's delight
Monahans Sandhills State Park
Balmorhea State Park

stairs was found on the wall of the saloon. A sign painter carefully traced the old design in its original color.

Displays on the upper floors depict life in Pecos in the late 1800s. There is an old schoolroom complete with maps and textbooks, and several of the hotel's rooms have been restored. You won't want to miss the saloon where quick-draw Barney Riggs gunned down the two outlaws, either.

Speaking of gunfighters, one of the most famous of them all, Clay Allison, has a cemetery all to himself in the Pecos city park. Known as the "gentleman gunfighter," it was said he "never killed a man that did not need killing." No, Allison wasn't gunned down, he was killed in a freight wagon accident.

Also, part of the museum not to be missed is a replica of Judge Roy Bean's famed Jersey Lilly Saloon. If you don't know about the Judge, you don't know about "Law West of the Pecos." With a stiff neck from an unsuccessful hanging and a one-volume law library (Texas Statutes 1879) and no degree, the Judge dispensed instant and often cruel sentences to those frontier adventurers. In this land of strong men, the Judge was one of the strongest. No real western museum would be complete without a tribute to the "Hanging Judge."

Pecos claims to be the site of the very first rodeo. Cowboys from the Hashknife, the 101, the Mill Iron, and other ranches competed in some contests back in 1883, and since 1929 Pecos has recreated the event every year, usually around the Fourth of July.

Other towns claim the first rodeo, too, but one undeniable claim Pecos makes is that she grows the tastiest cantaloupes in the world. Their distinctive flavor is the result of a unique combination of sunshine, mineralized soil, and water, and they are shipped to customers all over the world. Pecos prides herself on being "a taste of the real west," and her attractions, such as the Orient, prove this claim correct, too.

The Fate
of Many
Old Hotels

Ghosts of a Bygone Era. . .

Hotel ghosts come in all shapes and sizes. Cities have their massive ghosts, and small towns have their own phantoms, but all of the ghosts have several things in common. They are in the oldest section of town, and even though they may now be in rags and tatters, once upon a time they had obviously been the queen of their domain. Nearly all of these old dowagers were built in the twenties, and they all bear a remarkable similarity. It is almost as though a single construction firm took the same set of plans to every town in Texas and built hotels. Occasionally the color of the brick varies, but the basic form is either the classic U-shape or just straight up and down. Decoration on the exterior is non-existent or very simple. The hotels appear, for the most part, to be just a functional place to rent a room.

But these hotels offered much more than just rooms. As an integral part of the town, they were the center of all the social and business activities. Nearly every important event in the town's history was somehow connected with the hotel.

Here is where friends, celebrities, and presidents and other dignitaries stayed. Often their impression of a town was the impression they received from the hotel. People seldom remember everyone they meet when they travel, but they never forget the hotel they stayed in. A good reception received at a hotel makes such an impact that most people return again and again to make the hotel a traditional place to stay.

Nothing lasts forever, not even traditions, and hotels that were once so essential to towns and cities now stand vacant and totally deserted, no longer needed for any purpose whatsoever. The passenger trains that created so many of them no longer arrive, the superhighways bypass them, and the business community has moved to the suburbs. Travelers now prefer the convenience of parking their cars at their motel door and sleeping in a room that looks exactly like every other room.

The following hotels are not all of the deserted ones in Texas, by any means, merely some of the oldest and best known. Many hotels have been demolished completely, such as the Scharbauer in Midland, the Hilton in Lubbock, the Baker in Dallas, and the Eagle in Eagle Pass. These ghosts, too, may face a similar fate, but until then, they just stand there with their faded signs, broken windows, and boarded-up doors contributing absolutely nothing to a society that once could not do without them.

Beaumont. Once the pride of Beaumont, the *La Salle* has recently been purchased, and there was a report in the newspaper that she will be restored to her 1928 splendor.

Big Spring. Rising high above the plains of West Texas, the 15-story *Settles Hotel* is prime material for restoration. Called a "gem of modernistic architecture" during the grand opening in 1930, the hotel quickly fell victim to the Depression. She is now being offered for sale.

Boerne. The *Ye Kendall Inn* is more than 125 years old, and was once an important stage stop. She is now a private residence.

Colorado City. The *Baker* has nothing but cracked stucco walls, broken windows, and every other feature of a hotel in total abandonment.

Comfort. The *Faust* is closed except for a few rooms being used as a flower shop, but the stone structure is in excellent condition and the outside trim is freshly painted.

Eastland. The *Village*, originally the Conley, still stands forlornly on the Main Street of Eastland. Tourists come to admire the gorgeous stamp window in the Post Office and to see the remains of "Old Rip," the horned toad found alive in the cornerstone of the courthouse after 31 years, but no one seems to care about the hotel.

El Paso. The same owners of the Paso del Norte own the *Cortez*. Once one of El Paso's finest, she is under study for a complete renovation.

Galveston. Just off the Strand is the *Panama*. Everyone comes to stroll this historic part of Galveston, but the old derelict Panama is often missed.

Garrison. The *Wiley* was one of the best known railroad hotels in this part of East Texas. This white frame, two-story building has been vacant for many years and is now for sale.

Houston. There was a time when the *Rice Hotel* was Houston. As long as her original owner, Jesse Jones, was alive, her fame was known all over the country. This is where celebrities stayed, and this is where Houston's big business deals were made. Since she is on the National Register of Historic Places, the Rice will be preserved. Recently purchased by the West German firm, Rovi Development Corporation, the Rice may once again have a grand future.

Lufkin. Built in 1922, the 110-room, five-story *Angelina* has closed its doors, apparently for good. She was once one of the best hotels in East Texas.

Marshall. Right in the center of town, with her blond brick dirty and stained, the *Marshall Hotel* stands empty and the property of the First National Bank of Marshall.

Mineral Wells. Perhaps this is one of the saddest of the ghost stories. The 450-room *Baker Hotel* was once renowned all over the United States. Opening in 1929, her famous guests were Joe E. Brown, Jean Harlow, and even Bonnie and Clyde. Mineral Wells was one of the biggest health spas in the country, and famous for its "Crazy Waters." Also famous was its magnificent hotel with "the nation's finest therapeutic bath and massage service." Closed in 1963, she enjoyed a brief resurgence from 1965 to 1972. Empty since then, she is still one of the most gorgeous of the ghosts.

The original owners of this Baker Hotel also owned the Baker in Dallas. With hope, the Baker of Mineral Wells will escape the fate of the Baker in Dallas.

Ranger. Once the center of one of Texas' biggest oil booms, Ranger is now a small agricultural community with no need for its *Gholson Hotel.* A few stores exist on the first floor, but the rest is in ruins.

Tyler. Tyler is as famous for its hotel as it is for its roses, but the *Blackstone Hotel* stands in the way of progress. There is talk of tearing her down for a parking lot.

Uvalde. The *Kinkaid* has offered hospitality to John Nance Garner, Dana Andrews, Eddie Rickenbacker, Richard Widmark, Ronald Reagan, and Lyndon Johnson. Now closed, the property is for sale.

Waco. One of the oldest of the deserted hotels is the *Raleigh*, built in 1912. She was a social and commercial "hub" for many years, including the World War I years when Waco was a great military training center. The present owners are trying to obtain financing for a renovation.

Waxahachie. The *Rogers* is also an old 1912 hotel and has the un- usual addition of a swimming pool in the basement. When baseball teams trained in Waxahachie they lived in the Rogers—the Detroit Tigers in 1917 and 1918, the Cincinnati Reds in 1919, the Chicago White Sox in 1920, and Kansas City in 1921.

Wichita Falls. Remodeled into a hotel in 1926 from an old 1912 bank building, the *Holt* was patterned after the then famous Baker in Dallas. Closed since 1955, there is a movement underway to "re- cycle" the *Holt* as part of a general development plan for Wichita Falls' Depot Square Historical District.

These silent, broken monuments to a bygone era are just pathetic reminders of a way of life that no longer fits into the present. For most of them, the future is very bleak. Restoration and refurbishing costs are absolutely staggering. Many of the people who love old hotels do not have the financing available to renovate them, and large corporations are not very interested in a hotel that would cost more to restore than it would to build anew. Ironic as it seems, it is even too costly in some instances to tear them down and forget them completely. So here the old ladies stand, faded and on the brink of ruin, without much hope of rescue. Who knows, maybe some wealthy, concerned person will come along and see their grand possibilities under all the dirt and grime and restore them to their former glories. If that happens, we would indeed be the better for it.

Quite a few historic hotels have escaped the death-knell and continue to function in other capacities. Devotees of old buildings have salvaged the basic structures and converted the interiors for other uses. In a way it is sad that there is no longer any reason to maintain them as hotels, but at least they have not been torn down and forgotten completely.

One of the most popular conversions of these old hotels is into office buildings. The Southern Hotel in Llano, once a stage stop, underwent a painstaking restoration and now houses lovely offices for a hardware firm. And the old red brick Llano Hotel is now an annex to the courthouse.

Built in 1930 in anticipation of an oil boom that never materialized, the El Paisano Hotel in Marfa is a Spanish Baroque marvel. Once the finest hotel between El Paso and San Antonio, she is still remarkably well preserved. She has been remodeled into condominiums, shops, and a restaurant, but nearly all are vacant. She may soon be another ghost. The Holland Hotel, erected in 1912 in the Spanish Colonial style for Alpine's cattle baron, John A. Holland, was restored in 1973 as offices for various Alpine firms.

A really fantastic job of hotel restoration into offices and businesses was done with the Park Plaza Hotel in Sequine. Constructed in 1915 for $75,000, the Park Plaza is listed on the National Register of Historic Places and will no doubt be one of the most prestigious businesss addresses in Seguin. On a smaller scale, Floyd Addington of Jasper has taken the old 1910 Belle-Jim Hotel and made her into his private law firm.

Another practical use for old hotels is to donate them to schools to be used as dormitories. The BrownTowner in Brownwood is the Sid Richardson Hall for Men at Howard Payne University. Cisco's Victor Hotel has become part of Cisco Junior College, and Longview's Downtowner Hotel belongs to LeTourneau College.

In several cases Historical Societies have saved hotels from rack and ruin. The Schmitz Hotel, constructed in 1851, is said to have been the first hotel in Texas with running water. On the square of New Braunfels, her 1862 register listed Governor Sam Houston, Jefferson Davis, and Robert E. Lee. The Historical Society currently uses her as a center for their activities. The Fanthrope Inn in Anderson has been steeped in Texas history since her construction in 1834. In 1845, Anderson, the Vice-President of the Republic, died here. She has been acquired by the State of Texas to be restored as a museum. Another grand restoration job done by a historical society is the P. A. Smith Hotel in Navasota. Built in 1876, she has been placed on the National Register of Historic Places, and will serve Grimes County as an office building and a community center.

The ancient Keystone Hotel is still standing on Second Street in Lampasas. This 1870 stagestop was restored in 1978 to house the Lampasas Savings and Loan Association. Another hotel turned bank is the El Capitan in Van Horn. This mission-style white stucco

. . .and Those That Have Survived

hotel was the finest stopping place in Van Horn in the twenties and thirties, and has now become the Van Horn State Bank.

Banks, offices, restaurants, museums, dormitories—all are obvious uses of bankrupt hotel properties. Unfortunately, not all defunct hotels lend themselves to any other operation, so those gallant survivors that can still perform a service to their community are very lucky indeed. Texas and its historic buildings are extremely fortunate to have so many concerned citizens who want to keep their old traditional buildings and preserve them in some useful form.